Water-Quality and Flow Data, Chulitna River Basin, Southwest Alaska, October 2009–June 2012

By Timothy P. Brabets

Prepared in cooperation with the National Park Service

Open File Report 2013–1009

U.S. Department of the Interior
U.S. Geological Survey

U.S. Department of the Interior
KEN SALAZAR, Secretary

U.S. Geological Survey
Marcia K. McNutt, Director

U.S. Geological Survey, Reston, Virginia: 2013

For more information on the USGS—the Federal source for science about the Earth, its natural and living resources, natural hazards, and the environment, visit http://www.usgs.gov or call 1–888–ASK–USGS.

For an overview of USGS information products, including maps, imagery, and publications, visit http://www.usgs.gov/pubprod

To order this and other USGS information products, visit http://store.usgs.gov

Suggested citation:
Brabets, T.P., 2013, Water-quality and flow data, Chulitna River basin, Southwest Alaska, October 2009–June 2012: U.S. Geological Survey Open-File Report 2013–1009, 30 p.

Contents

Abstract 1

Introduction...1

    Purpose and Scope 4

Description of Study Area 4

Water-Quality Data 5

    Water-Quality Samples 5

    Continuous-Records of Dissolved Oxygen, pH, Specific Conductance, Turbidity, and Water
        Temperature...5

Flow Data...5

Acknowledgments..6

References Cited...6

Figures

1. Map showing location of Lake Clark National Park and Preserve and the
   Chulitna River basin, southwest Alaska... 2

2. Digital elevation map showing Lake Clark and Chulitna River basins and major
   river basins, southwest Alaska 3

3. Map showing locations of sampling sites, Chulitna River basin, southwest
   Alaska 4

Tables

1. Description of data-collection sites, Chulitna River basin, southwest Alaska 8
2. Analyses of water samples collected at USGS streamflow-gaging station 15298040, Chulitna River 5 miles above mouth, near Port Alsworth, Alaska, March 2010–June 2012 8
3. Summary of standard analytical methods and associated references used in this study 9
4. Physical field parameters measured at surface-water sites in the Chulitna River basin, Alaska, March 2010–June 2012 10
5. Concentrations of major ions in water samples collected at USGS streamflow-gaging station 15298040, Chulitna River 5 miles above mouth, near Port Alsworth, Alaska, March 2010–June 2012 11
6. Dissolved trace-element concentrations in water samples collected at USGS streamflow-gaging station 15298040, Chulitna River 5 miles above mouth, near Port Alsworth, Alaska, March 2010–June 2012 12
7. Concentrations of nutrients, dissolved organic carbon, and suspended sediment in water samples collected at USGS streamflow-gaging station 15298040, Chulitna River 5 miles above mouth, near Port Alsworth, Alaska, March 2010–June 2012. 13
8. Results from a blank sample collected at USGS streamflow-gaging station 15298040, Chulitna River 5 miles above mouth, near Port Alsworth, Alaska, August 18, 2010 13
9. Results from a replicate sample collected at USGS streamflow-gaging station 15298040, Chulitna River 5 miles above mouth, near Port Alsworth, Alaska, March 9, 2011 14
10. Water temperature data for USGS streamflow-gaging station 15298040, Chulitna River 5 miles above mouth, near Port Alsworth, Alaska, water years 2010 and 2011 15
11. Dissolved oxygen data for USGS streamflow-gaging station 15298040, Chulitna River 5 miles above mouth, near Port Alsworth, Alaska, water years 2010 and 2011 21
12. pH data for USGS streamflow-gaging station 15298040, Chulitna River 5 miles above mouth, near Port Alsworth, Alaska, water years 2010 and 2011 23
13. Specific conductance data for USGS streamflow-gaging station 15298040, Chulitna River 5 miles above mouth, near Port Alsworth, Alaska, water years 2010 and 2011 25
14. Turbidity data for USGS streamflow-gaging station 15298040, Chulitna River 5 miles above mouth, near Port Alsworth, Alaska, water years 2010 and 2011 27
15. Discharge data for USGS streamflow-gaging station 15298040, Chulitna River 5 miles above mouth, near Point Alsworth, Alaska, water years 2010 and 2011 ... 29

Conversion Factors, Datums, and Abbreviations and Acronyms

Conversion Factors

Multiply	By	To obtain
Length		
inch (in.)	2.54	centimeter (cm)
inch (in.)	25.4	millimeter (mm)
foot (ft)	0.3048	meter (m)
mile (mi)	1.609	kilometer (km)
Weight		
ounce (oz)	28.35	gram (g)
pound (lb)	0.4536	kilogram (kg)
Area		
square mile (mi^2)	259.0	hectare (ha)
square mile (mi^2)	2.590	square kilometer (km^2)
Flow rate		
cubic foot per second (ft^3/s)	0.02832	cubic meter per second (m^3/s)

Temperature in degrees Celsius (°C) may be converted to degrees Fahrenheit (°F) as follows:

$$°F=(1.8×°C)+32.$$

Specific conductance is given in microsiemens per centimeter at 25 degrees Celsius (µS/cm at 25 °C).

Concentrations of chemical constituents in water are given either in milligrams per liter (mg/L) or micrograms per liter (µg/L).

Datums

Vertical coordinate information is referenced to the North American Vertical Datum of 1929 (NAVD 29).

Horizontal coordinate information is referenced to the North American Datum of 1927 (NAD 27).

Altitude, as used in this report, refers to distance above the vertical datum.

Abbreviations and Acronyms

FNU	formazin Nephelometric units
LACL	Lake Clark National Park and Preserve
NFM	U.S. Geological Survey, National Field Manual
NWIS	U.S. Geological Survey, National Water Information System
USGS	U.S. Geological Survey

Water-Quality and Flow Data, Chulitna River Basin, Southwest Alaska, October 2009–June 2012

By Timothy P. Brabets

Abstract

The Chulitna River basin in southwest Alaska drains an area of about 1,160 square miles, with the lower 158 square miles of the basin in Lake Clark National Park and Preserve. Water from this basin influences Lake Clark ecosystems that support salmon that, in part, sustain the Bristol Bay fishery. An area of about 391 square miles in the upper part of the Chulitna River basin has been staked for mining development (1,670 claims), and a proposed large scale copper-gold-molybdenum mine (Pebble Mine) lies adjacent to the Chulitna River drainage. The U.S. Geological Survey in cooperation with the National Park Service conducted a water-quality assessment of the Chulitna River from October 2009 to June 2012. Discrete water-quality samples and continuous-records of dissolved oxygen, pH, specific conductance, turbidity, water-stage, and water temperature data were collected from the Chulitna River. In addition, four miscellaneous sites were visited five times during 2010–12 to measure flow and water-quality parameters.

Introduction

The Chulitna River basin in southwest Alaska is part of the Lake Clark basin in Lake Clark National Park and Preserve (LACL), Alaska (figs. 1–2). The basin supports a variety of aquatic and terrestrial life that depends on high-quality aquatic ecosystems. Fish and wildlife from this area support subsistence harvests by residents of the local communities of Iliamna, Newhalen, Port Alsworth, and Nondalton (Morris, 1986; Fall and others, 1996; Krieg and others, 2005). Fish species present within the basin include northern pike, Arctic grayling and char, burbot, longnose suckers, humpback and round whitefish, least cisco, nine-spine stickleback, slimy sculpin, sockeye salmon, occasional Chinook salmon, and Dolly Varden (Russell, 1980). The Chulitna River provides the only known spawning habitat for humpback whitefish and least cisco in the Lake Clark basin (Woody and Young, 2007). Humpback whitefish are the second most important fish harvested by subsistence users in the region after salmon (Fall and others, 1996; Krieg and others, 2005). Terrestrial wildlife within the drainage include grizzly bear, moose, caribou, and beaver.

The legislative purpose of LACL mandates that the park "….protect the watershed necessary for perpetuation of the red salmon fishery; … and maintain unimpaired…wild rivers, lakes, waterfalls…in their natural state" (Alaska National Interest Lands Conservation Act, 1980). The number-one natural resource priority for the park is to collect information needed to protect aquatic resources critical for the freshwater part of the salmon life cycle, including baseline information on water-quality and basic habitat characteristics.

Potential mining activity in the region poses a possible threat to the water quality and fisheries habitat in the Chulitna River basin. An area of about 391 mi^2 in the upper part of Chulitna River basin (fig. 3) has been staked for mining development (1,670 claims), and a proposed large scale copper-gold-molybdenum mine (Pebble Mine) lies adjacent to the Chulitna River drainage (fig. 1). Owners of the Pebble Mine are proceeding with a program of core drilling and environmental sampling, with plans to submit applications for permits by 2013 and to start mining operations several years later. The Pebble Mine deposit is currently estimated at 80.6 billion pounds (lb) of copper, 107.4 million ounces (oz) of gold, and 5.6 billion pounds (lb) of molybdenum (Pebble Partnership, 2012), and has an estimated value ranging from $300 to $500 billion (American Association for the Advancement of Science, 2011). To date, the Pebble Partnership has spent more than $100 million to support development of the deposit (Pebble Partnership, 2012). If permitted, the Pebble Mine may include the largest open-pit mine in North America, an underground mine, a 700-ft-high tailings dam, a tailings pond, a mill, a 100-mi transportation corridor with a road and slurry pipeline, a port facility on Cook Inlet, and extensive support facilities (Chambers, 2007; Hauser, 2007; Moran, 2007).

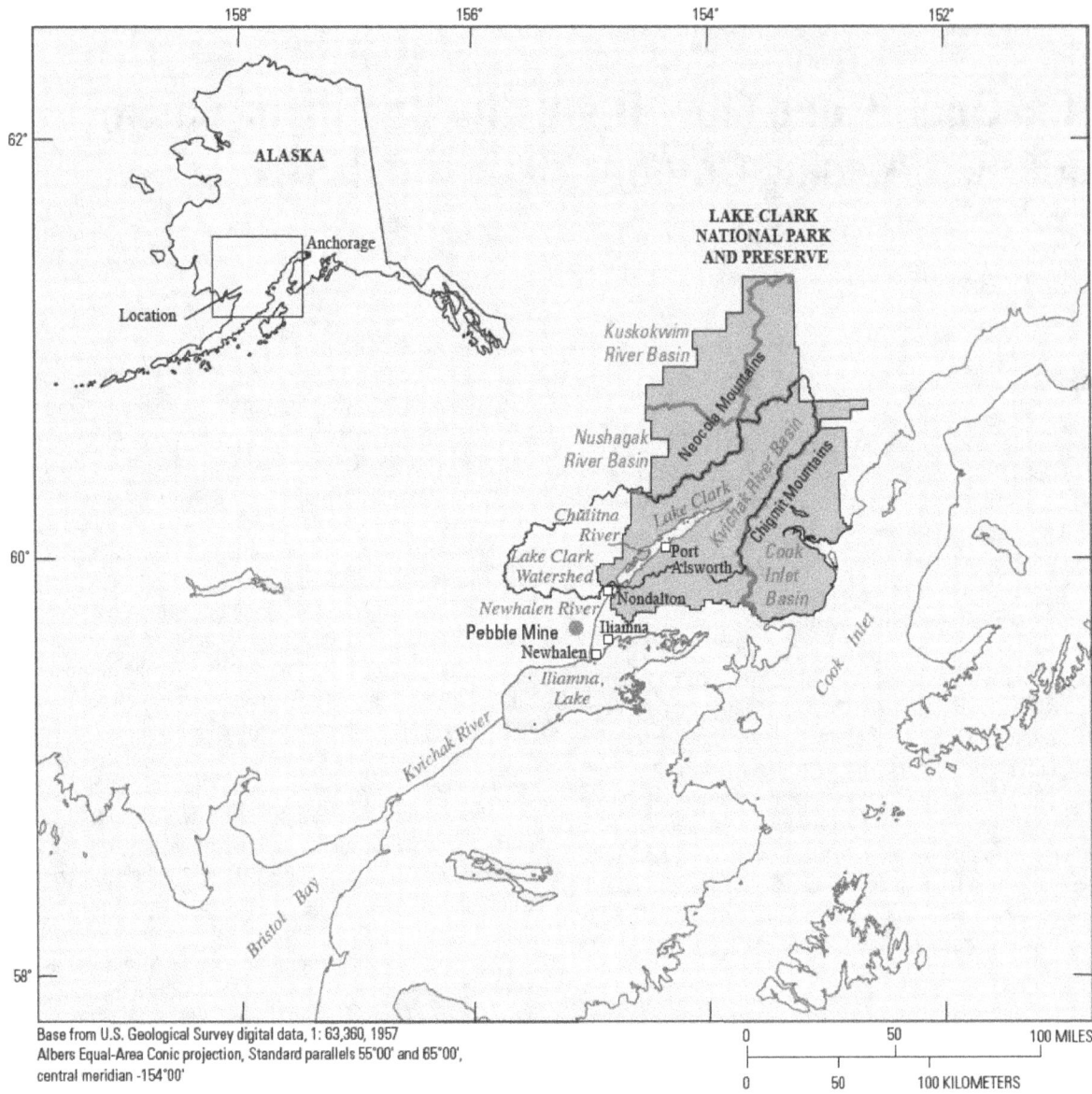

Figure 1.   Location of Lake Clark National Park and Preserve and the Chulitna River basin, southwest Alaska.

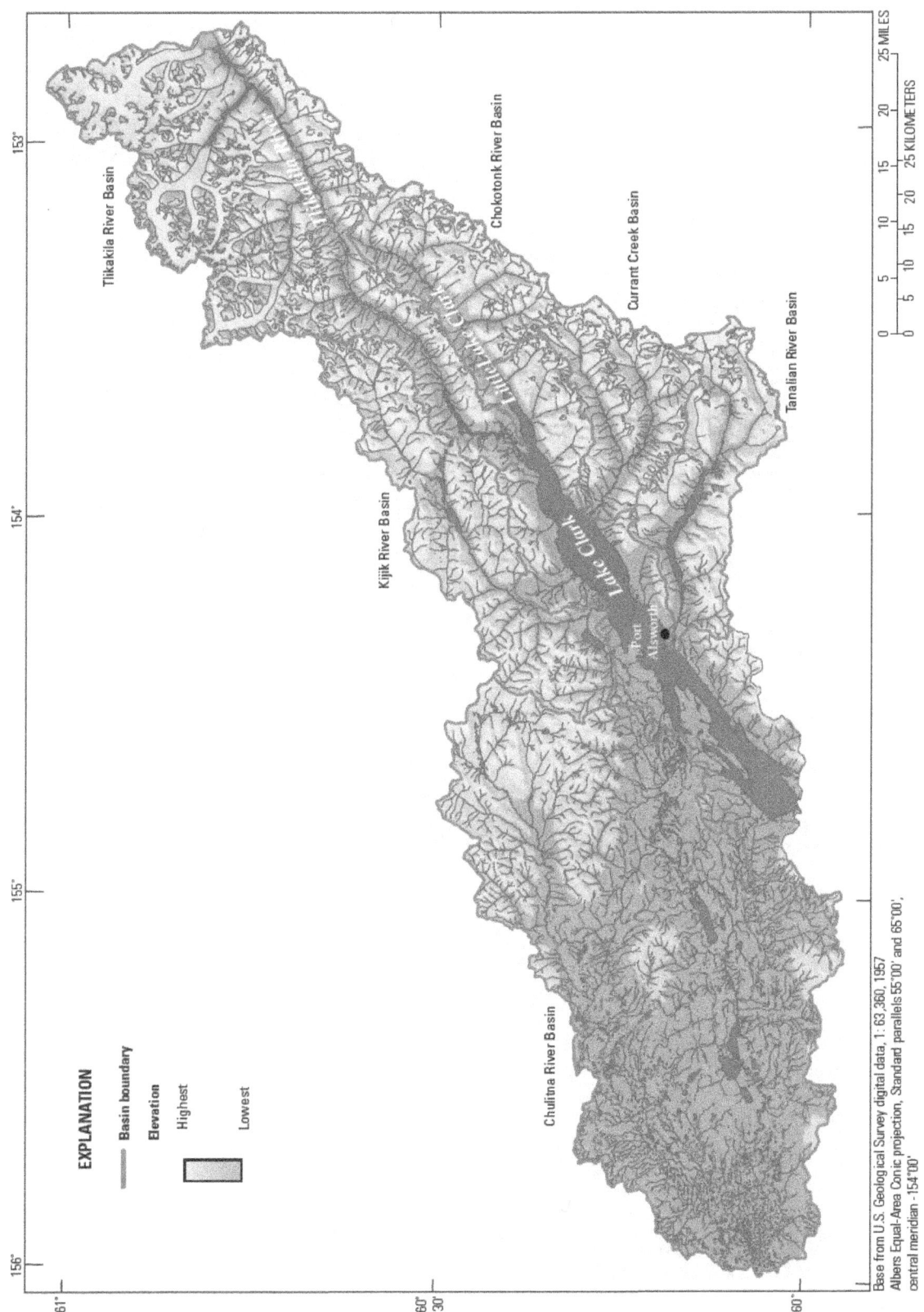

Base from U.S. Geological Survey digital data, 1: 63,360, 1957
Albers Equal-Area Conic projection, Standard parallels 55°00' and 65°00',
central meridian -154°00'

Figure 2. Lake Clark and Chulitna River basins and major river basins, southwest Alaska.

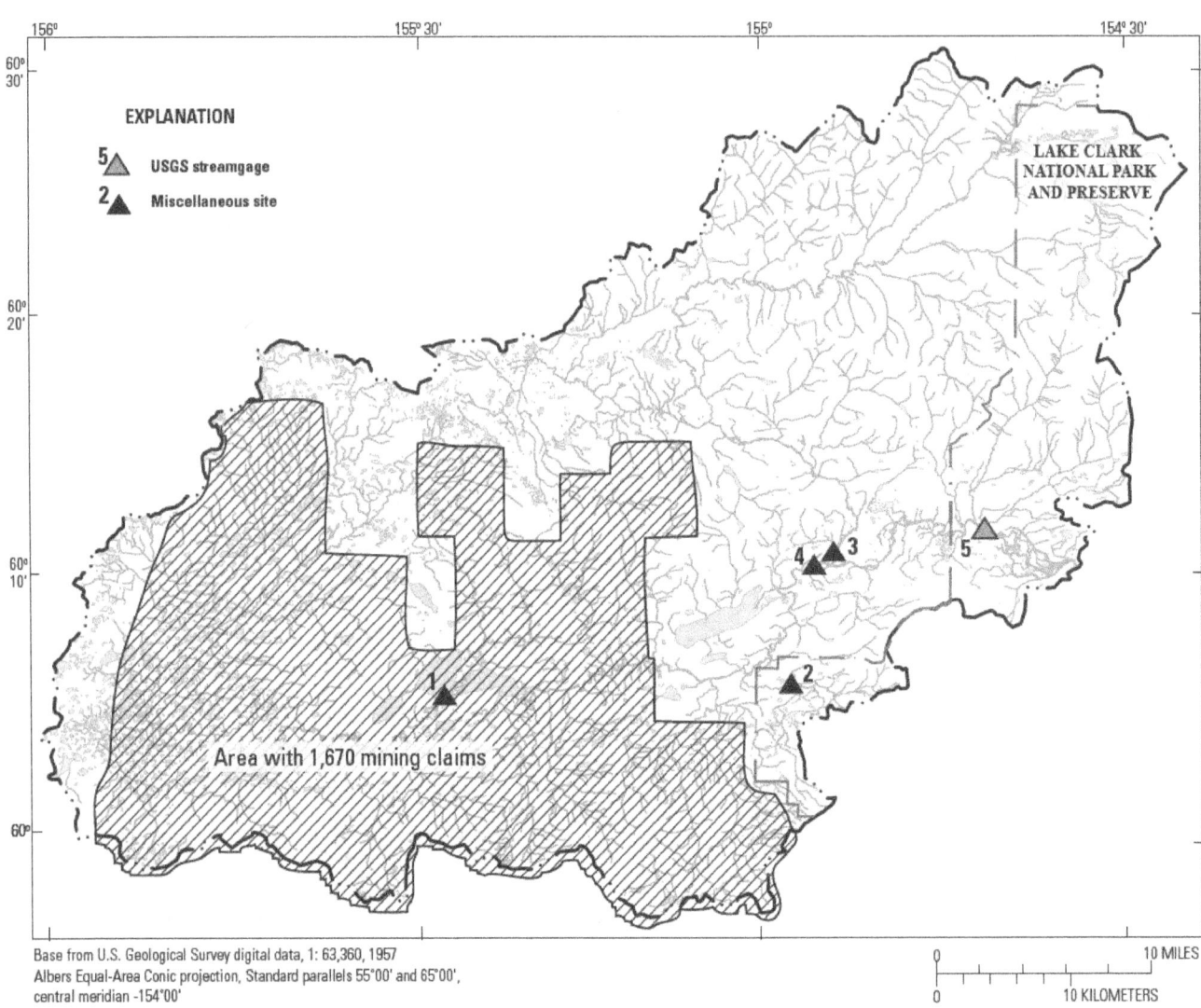

Figure 3.   Locations of sampling sites, Chulitna River basin, southwest Alaska.

Although mining currently (2012) is not taking place in the Chulitna River basin, the National Park Service still is responsible for ensuring that waters entering Lake Clark National Park and Preserve remain at a quality level that supports native species. The scale and location of the proposed mining claims could pose a threat to the water quality and fish habitat of the Chulitna River basin and downstream ecosystems because the Chulitna River provides between 20 and 30 percent of the total inflow to Lake Clark (Brabets, 2002).

Purpose and Scope

This report contains water-quality and flow data collected by the U.S. Geological Survey (USGS) from October 2009 to June 2012 at USGS gaging station 15298040, and at four miscellaneous sites in the Chulitna River basin (fig. 3 and table 1). Water-quality data consist of discrete water samples

collected at various times during the hydrologic year at USGS streamgage 15298040, and continuous water-quality monitoring of dissolved oxygen, pH, specific conductance, turbidity, and water temperature at the gaging station. Field parameters were collected at four additional miscellaneous sites. Flow data consist of periodic streamflow measurements and continuous streamflow monitoring. All data are stored in the USGS National Water Information System (NWIS).

Description of Study Area

Lake Clark National Park and Preserve is in south-central and southwest Alaska (fig. 1). The park is about 6,300 mi^2 in area and straddles several river basins. About one-third of the park is in the Cook Inlet basin of south-central Alaska (fig. 1). Streams and rivers in this section of the park flow east into Cook Inlet. The remaining two-thirds of the park are in the Kvichak, Kuskokwim, and Nushagak River basins of southwest Alaska. Streams and rivers in the Kvichak and Nushagak River basins flow southwest, eventually entering Bristol Bay. For sockeye salmon *(Oncorhynchus nerka)*, the Kvichak River basin is one of the most productive basins in Alaska. Each year, an estimated 1.5 to 6 million sockeye enter the Lake Clark basin through the Newhalen River to spawn in the many streams in the park.

The Lake Clark basin (fig. 2) drains 2,940 mi^2. In addition to six major rivers that flow into Lake Clark, there are numerous small glacier-fed streams originating in the Chigmit and Neocola Mountains and clearwater streams originating in the foothills and lowlands that flow into Lake Clark. The Chulitna River basin is 1,160 mi^2 in area (at the mouth), and is the largest basin in the Lake Clark basin. Mean basin slope is 7 percent, mean annual precipitation is 26 in., average altitude is 1,080 ft, no glaciers are present, and lakes occupy an area of 35.5 mi^2 of the basin (Brabets, 2002). Mesozoic sedimentary rock is the major rock type, and the major soils are spodosols, histosols, and andisols. Low and tall shrubs are the major vegetation. A previous study by Brabets (2002) indicates that the Chulitna River provides 20–30 percent of the inflow to Lake Clark.

Water-Quality Data

The following sections describe water sample-collection techniques, analytical methods, and flow collection techniques used at the sampling location on the Chulitna River. A summary of site characteristics (latitude, longitude, drainage area, and altitude) is provided in table 1, and the site locations are shown in figure 3. All data discussed in this section also are available from the U.S. Geological Survey (2012).

Water-Quality Samples

Water-quality samples were collected at various times at the USGS streamgage. Samples collected in March 2010, 2011, and 2012 were collected through the river ice. The final sample was collected in June 2012. In total, 12 samples were collected. A broad range of constituents were measured, including field parameters, major ions, dissolved trace elements, nutrients, and suspended sediment (table 2).

Water-quality collection and processing procedures followed USGS National Field Manual (NFM) protocols (U.S. Geological Survey, variously dated). A two-person minimum field team collected samples to reduce the opportunity for contamination of low-concentration analytes, following the protocols of Horowitz and others (1994) and Shelton (1994). Sampling and processing equipment was cleaned prior to each field trip following USGS NFM procedures.

The USGS National Water-Quality Laboratory in Denver, Colorado, analyzed all discrete water samples for dissolved and whole-water constituents using standard USGS methods and quality-assurance practices (Fishman and Friedman, 1989; Patton and Truitt, 1992; Fishman, 1993; Garbarino and others, 2006). A summary of the standard analytical methods used and associated references is provided in table 3. Analytical results are presented in tables 4–7.

The four miscellaneous sites were visited a total of five times during the data-collection period. Sites were visited in March 2010, 2011, and 2012, a low-flow, ice-covered period, and twice in the summer (July 2010 and August 2011) during average flow or above average flow conditions. At the time of each visit, a discharge measurement was made and water-quality field parameters were measured—dissolved oxygen, pH, specific conductance, turbidity, and water temperature. Data for these sites are presented in table 4.

During the data-collection period, quality-assurance and quality-control protocols were used. A sample containing blank water was collected with the August 18, 2010 sample, and a replicate sample was collected with the March 9, 2011 sample. Results from these 2010 and 2011 samples are given in tables 8 and 9, respectively.

Continuous-Records of Dissolved Oxygen, pH, Specific Conductance, Turbidity, and Water Temperature

At the USGS streamgage 15298040, a Yellow Springs Instrument Model 6920 sonde was installed during the open-water season in water years 2010 and 2011 to collect continuous dissolved oxygen, pH, specific conductance, turbidity, and water temperature data. Data were collected every 15 minutes. This period generally lasted from late May to the end of September. Water temperature also was collected from the stage sensor; therefore, these data are available for the entire water year. Water- quality data were compiled using methods outlined in Wagner and others (2006) and are shown in tables 10–14.

Flow Data

A sensor was installed in October 2009 at the streamgage to collect continuous stage data. Using methods outlined by Turnispeed and Sauer (2010), a number of discharge measurements were made over a range of flows. A stage-discharge relation was then developed to compute daily discharge at the streamgage. Discharge data for water years 2010 and 2011 are shown in table 15.

Acknowledgments

This study was funded by the National Park Service/U.S. Geological Survey Water-Quality Partnership Program. Special thanks go to Dan Young of LACL at Port Alsworth who arranged housing for USGS personnel during sampling trips, boats to access the Chulitna River gaging station, and the use of the park plane to access the miscellaneous sites.

References Cited

Alaska National Interest Lands Conservation Act, 1980, 16 U.S.C 3101 et seq. (1988), December 2, 1980, Stat. 2371, Pub. L. 96–487.

American Association for the Advancement of Science, 2011, Proposed Pebble Mine has Alaskan community focused on critical science and policy issues: American Association for the Advancement of Science news release, accessed October 22, 2012, at http://www.aaas.org/news/releases/2011/1018arctic_div_pebble.shtml.

Brabets, T.P., 2002, Water quality of the Tlikakila River and five major tributaries to Lake Clark, Lake Clark National Park and Preserve, Alaska 1999–2001: U.S. Geological Survey Water-Resources Investigations Report 2002–4127, 29 p. (Also available at http://pubs.er.usgs.gov/publication/wri024127.)

Brenton, R.W., and Arnett, T.L., 1993, Methods of analysis by the U.S. Geological Survey National Water Quality Laboratory–Determination of dissolved organic carbon by UV-promoted persulfate of oxidation and infrared spectrometry: U.S. Geological Survey Open-File Report 92–480, 12 p. (Also available at http://pubs.er.usgs.gov/publication/ofr92480.)

Chambers, D.M., 2007, Pebble engineering geology—Discussion of issues: Center for Science in Public Participation, accessed October 22, 2012, at http://fish4thefuture.com/pdfs/Pebble%20Engineering%20Geology%20-%20Chambers%20Sep07.pdf.

Fall, J.A., Chythlook, M.B., Schichnes, J.C., and Morris, J.M., 1996, An overview of the harvest and use of freshwater fish by the communities of the Bristol Bay region, southwest Alaska: Alaska Department of Fish and Game, Division of Subsistence, Technical Paper Series, Technical Paper No. 166, 171 p.

Fishman, M.J., ed., 1993, Methods of analysis by the U.S. Geological Survey National Water-Quality Laboratory—Determination of inorganic and organic constituents in water and fluvial sediments: U.S. Geological Survey Open-File Report 93–125, 217 p. (Also available at http://pubs.er.usgs.gov/publication/ofr93125.)

Fishman, M.J., and Friedman, L.C., eds., 1989, Method for determination of inorganic substances in water and fluvial sediments: U.S. Geological Survey Techniques of Water-Resources Investigations, book 5, chap. A1, 545 p. (Also available at http://pubs.er.usgs.gov/publication/twri05A1.)

Fishman, M.J., Raese, J.W., Gerlitz, C. N., and Husband, R.A., 1994, U.S. Geological Survey approved inorganic and organic methods for the analysis of water and fluvial sediment, 1954–94: U.S. Geological Survey Open-File Report 94–351, 55 p. (Also available at http://pubs.er.usgs.gov/publication/ofr94351.)

Garbarino, J.R., Kanagy, L.K., and Cree, M.E., 2006, Determination of elements in natural-water, biota, sediment and soil samples using collision-reaction cell inductively coupled plasma-mass spectrometry: U.S. Geological Survey Techniques and Methods, book 5, sec. B, chap. 1, 87 p. (Also available at http://pubs.er.usgs.gov/publication/tm5B1.)

Guy, H.P., 1969, Laboratory theory and methods for sediment analysis: U.S. Geological Survey Techniques of Water-Resources Investigations, book 5, chapter C1, 58 p.

Hauser, W.J., 2007, Potential impacts of the proposed Pebble Mine on fish habitat and fishery resources of Bristol Bay: Fisheries Research and Consulting web site, accessed October 22, 2012, at http://fish4thefuture.com/pdfs/Pebble%20Fish%20Habitat%20Report%20-%20Hauser%20Sep%2007.pdf.

Horowitz, A.J., Demas, C.R., Fitzgerald, K.K., Miller, T.L., and Rickert, D.A., 1994, U.S. Geological Survey protocol for the collection and processing of surface-water samples for the subsequent determination of inorganic constituents in filtered water: U.S. Geological Survey Open-File report 94-539, 57 p. (Also available at http://pubs.er.usgs.gov/publication/ofr94539.)

Krieg, T., Chythlook, M.B., Coiley-Kenner, P., Holen, D., Kamletz, K., and Nicholson, H., 2005, Freshwater fish harvest and use in communities of the Kvichak watershed: Juneau, Alaska, Alaska Department of Fish and Game, Division of Subsistence, Technical Paper 297.

Moran, R.E., 2007, Pebble hydrogeology and geochemistry issues: Fisheries Research and Consulting web site accessed October 22, 2012, at http://fish4thefuture.com/pdfs/Moran_Hydrogeology_Geochemistry_8_9_07.pdf.

Morris, J.M., 1986, Subsistence production and exchange in the Iliamna Lake region, southwest Alaska, 1982–1983: Juneau, Alaska, Alaska Department of Fish and Game, Division of Subsistence, Technical Paper No. 136, 187 p.

Patton, C.J., and Truitt, E.P., 1992, Methods of analysis by the U.S. Geological Survey National Water Quality Laboratory—Determination of total phosphorus by a Kjeldahl digestion method and an automated colorimetric finish that includes dialysis: U.S. Geological Survey Open-File Report 92–146, 39 p. (Also available at http://pubs.er.usgs.gov/publication/ofr92146.)

Patton, C.J., and Truitt, E.P., 2000, Methods of analysis by the U.S. Geological Survey National Water Quality Laboratory—Determination of ammonium plus organic nitrogen by a Kjeldahl digestion method and an automated photometric finish that includes digest cleanup by gas diffusion: U.S. Geological Survey Open-File Report 2000-170, 31 p. (Also available at http://pubs.er.usgs.gov/publication/ofr00170.)

Pebble Partnership, 2012, Prospecting the future: Pebble Partnership web site accessed October 22, 2012, at http://www.pebblepartnership.com/project.php.

Russell, R., 1980, A fisheries inventory of waters in the Lake Clark National Monument area: Alaska Department of Fish and Game, 124 p.

Shelton, L.R., 1994, Field guide for collecting and processing stream-water samples for the National Water-Quality Assessment Program: U.S. Geological Survey Open-File Report 94–455, 42 p. (Also available at http://pubs.er.usgs.gov/publication/ofr94455.)

Turnipseed, D.P., and Sauer, V.B., 2010, Discharge measurements at gaging stations—U.S. Geological Survey Techniques and Methods, book 3, chap. A8, 87 p. (Also available at http://pubs.er.usgs.gov/publication/tm3A8.)

U.S. Geological Survey, variously dated, National field manual for the collection of water-quality data: U.S. Geological Survey Techniques of Water-Resources Investigations, book 9, chaps. A1-A9. (Also available at http://pubs.er.usgs.gov/publication/twri09.)

U.S. Geological Survey, 2012, USGS water data for Alaska: U.S. Geological Survey National Water Information System web interface, accessed September 14, 2012, at http://waterdata.usgs.gov/ak/nwis/.

Wagner, R.J., Boulger, R.W., Oblinger, C.J., and Smith, B.A., 2006, Guidelines and standard procedures for continuous water-quality monitors—Station operation, record computation, and data reporting: U.S. Geological Survey Techniques and Methods, book 1, chap. D3, 51 p. (also available at http://pubs.er.usgs.gov/publication/tm1D3.)

Woody, C.A., and Young, D.Y., 2007, Life history and essential habitats of humpback whitefish in Lake Clark National Park, Kvichak River watershed, Alaska: Anchorage, U.S. Fish and Wildlife Service Office of Subsistence Management, Annual Report for Study FIS 05-403.

Table 1.   Description of data-collection sites, Chulitna River basin, southwest Alaska.

[**Site No.:** Location of Site No. is shown in figure 3. **Abbreviations:** USGS, U.S. Geological Survey; mi², square mile]

Site No.	USGS No.	Latitude/ longitude	Station name	Area (mi²)	Remarks
1	600524155254200	60°05'24" 155°25'42"	Chulitna River 0.4 mile above Nikabuna Lake, near Nondalton	335	Miscellaneous site
2	600610154570100	60°06'10" 154°57'01"	Hoknede Lake Creek 0.4 mile below Hoknede Lake, near Nondalton	15.3	Miscellaneous site
3	601049154540600	60°10'49" 154°54'06"	Koksetna River 0.1 mile above mouth, near Nondalton	375	Miscellaneous site
4	601050154544400	60°10'50" 154°54'44"	Chulitna River 0 3 mile above Koksetna River, near Nondalton	664	Miscellaneous site
5	15298040	60°12'16" 154°42'08"	Chulitna River 5 miles above mouth, near Port Alsworth	1,120	Continuous site

Table 2.   Analyses of water samples collected at USGS streamflow-gaging station 15298040, Chulitna River 5 miles above mouth, near Port Alsworth, Alaska, March 2010–June 2012.

[**Abbreviations:** C, degrees Celsius; µS/cm, microsiemens per centimeter at 25 degrees Celsius; mg/L, milligram per liter; FNU, Formazin nephelometric unit; ft³/s, cubic foot per second; µg/L, microgram per liter; mm, millimeter]

Water-quality parameter	Reporting level	Units	Water-quality parameter	Reporting level	Units
Field measurements of water			**Trace elements (µg/L)—Continued**		
Water temperature	0.5	°C	Cobalt	0.1090	
Specific conductance	1	µS/cm	Copper	1.0	
pH	0.1	unit	Iron	6	
Dissolved oxygen	0.1	mg/L	Lead	0.030	
Turbidity	0.1	FNU	Lithium	0.44	
Streamflow	0.1	ft³/s	Manganese	0.2272	
Major ions (mg/L)			Molybdenum	0.028	
			Nickel	0.12	
Alkalinity	8		Selenium	0.04	
Bicarbonate	1		Silver	0.010	
Calcium	0.044		Strontium	0.40	
Chloride	0.08		Thallium	0.02	
Dissolved solids	10		Uranium	0.008	
Fluoride	0.08		Vanadium	0.16	
Magnesium	0.016		Zinc	2.8	
Potassium	0.064		**Suspended sediment in water (mg/L)**		
Silica	0.058				
Sodium	0.10		Concentration	1	
Sulfate	0.18		Percent finer than 0.062 mm	1	
Trace elements (µg/L)			**Nutrients in water (mg/L)**		
Aluminum	3.4		Nitrogen, ammonia, dissolved	0.02	
Antimony	0.402		Nitrogen, ammonia+organic, dissolved	0.10	
Arsenic	0.044		Nitrogen, ammonia+organic, total	0.10	
Barium	0.14		Nitrogen, nitrite+nitrate, dissolved	0.016	
Beryllium	0.012		Nitrogen, nitrite, dissolved	0.002	
Boron	2.8		Phosphorus, dissolved	0.006	
Cadmium	0.02		Orthophosphorus, dissolved	0.008	
Chromium	0.12		Phosphorus, total	0.008	
			Dissolved organic carbon	0.66	

Table 3.   Summary of standard analytical methods and associated references used in this study.

[**Abbreviations:** Dis, dissolved; fet, fixed end-point; tot, total; IT, incremental titration; mm, millimeter]

Water-quality parameter	Reference	Analytical method
Solids, residue, dissolved	Fishman and others (1994)	Gravimetric, residue on evaporation at 180 C
Turbidity	Fishman and Friedman (1989)	Nephelometry
Oxygen, dissolved	U.S. Geological Survey (1997–99)	Amperometric
pH, whole water	U.S. Geological Survey (1997–99)	Electrometric electrode
Specific conductance	U.S. Geological Survey (1997–99)	Wheatstone Bridge
Major ions		
Calcium, dissolved	Fishman (1993)	Inductively Coupled Plasma–Atomic Emission Spectrometry
Magnesium, dissolved	Fishman (1993)	Inductively Coupled Plasma–Atomic Emission Spectrometry
Potassium, dissolved	Fishman and Friedman (1989)	Flame atomic absorption
Sodium, dissolved	Fishman (1993)	Inductively Coupled Plasma–Atomic Emission Spectrometry
Alkalinity, Dis fet lab, as $CaCO_3$	U.S. Geological Survey (1997–99)	Dissolved fixed end point titration
Alkalinity, Dis tot IT, field	U.S. Geological Survey (1997–99)	Dissolved incremental end point titration
Bicarbonate Dis IT, field	U.S. Geological Survey (1997–99)	Calculated
Chloride, dissolved	Fishman and Friedman (1989)	Ion chromatography
Fluoride, dissolved	Fishman and Friedman (1989)	Automated segmented flow-ion-selective electrode
Silica, dissolved	Fishman (1993)	Inductively Coupled Plasma–Atomic Emission Spectrometry
Sulfate, dissolved	Fishman and Friedman (1989)	Ion chromatography
Nutrients		
Nitrogen, ammonia, dissolved	Fishman (1993)	Colorimetry, automated segmented flow–salicylate-hypochlorite
Nitrogen, ammonia+organic, dissolved	Patton and Truitt (2000)	Colorimetry, automated segmented flow–Microkjeldahl digestion
Nitrogen, ammonia+organic, total	Fishman and others (1994)	Colorimetry, block digestor salicylate-hypochlorite
Nitrogen, nitrite+nitrate, dissolved	Fishman (1993)	Colorimetry, automated segmented flow–cadmium reduction-diazotization
Nitrogen, nitrate, dissolved	Fishman and Friedman (1989)	Ion chromatography
Phosphorus, dissolved	Patton and Truitt (1992)	Colorimetry, automated segmented flow–Microkjeldahl digestion
Orthophosphorus	Fishman (1993)	Colorimetry, automated segmented flow–phosphomolybdate
Phosphorus, total	Patton and Truitt (1992)	Colorimetry, automated segmented flow–Microkjeldahl digestion
Carbon, organic, dissolved (DOC)	Brenton and Arnett (1993)	Wet-chemical oxidation, nondispersive infrared detector
Trace elements		
Aluminum, dissolved	Garbarino and others (2006)	Inductively Coupled Plasma–Mass Spectrometry
Antimony, dissolved	Garbarino and others (2006)	Inductively Coupled Plasma–Mass Spectrometry
Arsenic, dissolved	Garbarino and others (2006)	Inductively Coupled Plasma–Mass Spectrometry
Barium, dissolved	Garbarino and others (2006)	Inductively Coupled Plasma–Mass Spectrometry
Beryllium, dissolved	Garbarino and others (2006)	Inductively Coupled Plasma–Mass Spectrometry
Boron, dissolved	Garbarino and others (2006)	Inductively Coupled Plasma–Mass Spectrometry
Cadmium, dissolved	Garbarino and others (2006)	Inductively Coupled Plasma–Mass Spectrometry
Chromium, dissolved	Garbarino and others (2006)	Inductively Coupled Plasma–Mass Spectrometry
Cobalt, dissolved	Garbarino and others (2006)	Inductively Coupled Plasma–Mass Spectrometry
Copper, dissolved	Garbarino and others (2006)	Inductively Coupled Plasma–Mass Spectrometry
Iron, dissolved	Fishman (1993)	Inductively Coupled Plasma–Atomic Emission Spectrometry
Lead, dissolved	Garbarino and others (2006)	Inductively Coupled Plasma–Mass Spectrometry
Lithium, dissolved	Garbarino and others (2006)	Inductively Coupled Plasma–Mass Spectrometry
Manganese, dissolved	Garbarino and others (2006)	Inductively Coupled Plasma–Mass Spectrometry
Molybdenum, dissolved	Garbarino and others (2006)	Inductively Coupled Plasma–Mass Spectrometry
Nickel, dissolved	Garbarino and others (2006)	Inductively Coupled Plasma–Mass Spectrometry
Selenium, dissolved	Garbarino and others (2006)	Inductively Coupled Plasma–Mass Spectrometry
Silver, dissolved	Garbarino and others (2006)	Inductively Coupled Plasma–Mass Spectrometry
Strontium, dissolved	Garbarino and others (2006)	Inductively Coupled Plasma–Mass Spectrometry
Thallium, dissolved	Garbarino and others (2006)	Inductively Coupled Plasma–Mass Spectrometry
Uranium, dissolved	Garbarino and others (2006)	Inductively Coupled Plasma–Mass Spectrometry
Vanadium, dissolved	Garbarino and others (2006)	Inductively Coupled Plasma–Mass Spectrometry
Zinc, dissolved	Garbarino and others (2006)	Inductively Coupled Plasma–Mass Spectrometry
Suspended-sediment		
Suspended-sediment	Guy (1969)	Evaporation
Percent finer than 0.062 mm	Guy (1969)	Pipet

Table 4.   Physical field parameters measured at surface-water sites in the Chulitna River basin, Alaska, March 2010–June 2012.

[Number in parentheses below constituent is number used by both U.S. Environmental Protection Agency and U.S. Geological Survey to identify parameters in computerized databases. Values represent the average of the cross section. Measurements were taken at four to five locations along the cross section. **Site No.:** Location of site No. is shown in figure 3. **Abbreviations:** ft³/s, cubic foot per second; mg/L, milligram per liter; µs/cm at 25 C, microsiemens per centimeter at 25 degrees Celsius; C, degrees Celsius; LED, light-emitting diode; nm, nanometer; FNU, Formazin Nephelometric Unit; <, less than; –, not measured]

Site No.	Date	Time	Streamflow (ft³/s) (00061)	Dissolved oxygen (mg/L) (00300)	pH (units) (00400)	Specific conductance (µs/cm at 25°C) (00095)	Water temperature (°C) (00010)	Turbidity, water, unfiltered, near infra-red LED light, 780–900 nm detection angle 90 ± 2.5 degrees (FNU) (63680)
				Chulitna River 0.4 mile above Nikabuna Lake, near Nondalton				
1	03-25-2010	1504	52	6.8	6.8	131	0.4	–
	07-22-2010	1725	791	10.1	7.4	62	11.3	13
	03-09-2011	1602	65	7.4	6.9	131	0.0	<2.0
	08-23-2011	1430	1,020	9.5	7.0	61	11.4	9.2
	03-14-2012	1325	88	9.4	7.0	122	0.0	<2
				Hoknede Lake Creek 0.4 mile below Hoknede Lake, near Nondalton				
2	03-24-2010	1410	2.9	9.5	6.8	63	1.4	–
	07-22-2010	1608	20	10.9	7.6	47	13.5	2.5
	03-09-2011	1334	2.7	10.3	6.9	68	0.6	<2.0
	08-23-2011	1720	24	10.7	7.5	43	14.4	<2.0
	03-13-2012	1600	3	9.6	6.6	41	0.4	<2
				Koksetna River 0.1 mile above mouth, near Nondalton				
3	03-25-2010	1215	109	13.0	7.4	97	0.0	–
	07-22-2010	1344	1,070	11.7	7.9	79	10.0	3.1
	03-08-2011	1535	76	13.3	7.4	98	0.0	<2.0
	08-24-2011	1341	1,310	12.0	7.6	79	8.0	<2.0
	03-12-2012	1730	159	14	7.3	91	0.0	<2
				Chulitna River 0.3 mile above Koksetna River, near Nondalton				
4	03-25-2010	1050	106	6.4	6.8	129	0.0	–
	07-22-2010	1445	1,100	10.5	7.7	65	12.4	4.8
	03-08-2011	1418	138	9.4	6.9	126	0.0	<2.0
	08-24-2011	1300	1,670	10.2	7.4	66	11.8	<2.0
	03-13-2012	1436	212	7.5	6.7	119	0.0	<2
				Chulitna River 5 miles above mouth, near Port Alsworth				
5	03-23-2010	1810	277	–	7.0	114	0.1	–
	05-25-2010	2046	2,230	12.6	7.5	59	9.7	4.1
	07-21-2010	1912	2,770	11.5	7.6	71	10.9	9.0
	08-18-2010	1531	5,830	10.7	7.3	57	10.0	5.1
	09-29-2010	1300	1,830	12.3	7.5	78	3.3	6.1
	03-09-2011	1100	331	10.7	6.9	108	0.0	<2.0
	05-26-2011	1752	2,580	12.1	7.5	63	7.8	8.4
	07-13-2011	1410	2,530	11.1	7.4	68	10.2	2.5
	08-24-2011	1656	3,190	11.5	7.4	72	10.2	<2.0
	09-27-2011	1728	1,960	12.0	7.3	76	7.0	<2.0
	03-14-2012	1545	457	9.9	7.0	105	0.0	<2.0
	06-19-2012	1408	3,480	11.5	7.5	66	10.3	7.0

Table 5. Concentrations of major ions in water samples collected at USGS streamflow-gaging station 15298040, Chulitna River 5 miles above mouth, near Port Alsworth, Alaska, March 2010–June 2012.

[Number in parentheses below constituent is number used by both U.S. Environmental Protection Agency and U.S. Geological Survey to identify parameters in computerized databases. Location of Site No. is shown in figure 3. All values in milligrams per liter. **Abbreviation:** E, estimated]

Date	Time	Alkalinity (39086)	Bicarbonate (00453)	Calcium (00915)	Chloride (00940)	Dissolved solids (70300)	Fluoride (00950)	Magnesium (00925)	Potassium (00935)	Silica (00955)	Sodium (00930)	Sulfate (00945)
				Site 5 – Chulitna River 5 miles above mouth, near Port Alsworth (15298040)								
03-23-2010	1810	46	56	14.5	0.808	66	0.080	2.48	0.694	12.0	2.66	8.43
05-25-2010	1530	23	28	7.38	.590	48	.084	1.39	.610	6.34	1.68	4.20
07-21-2010	1720	33	40	9.10	.348	61	E.058	1.77	.320	7.15	1.79	5.78
08-18-2010	1450	21	25	7.64	.345	46	E.049	1.48	.339	7.90	1.61	4.96
09-29-2010	1230	28	34	10.2	.497	51	E.061	1.88	.402	8.15	2.17	6.67
03-09-2011	1740	40	49	15.3	.709	66	.062	2.65	.632	11.8	2.72	8.80
05-26-2011	1740	22	27	8.43	.543	42	.049	1.54	.486	6.91	1.77	6.29
07-13-2011	1320	25	31	8.97	.380	50	.061	1.73	.318	8.03	1.86	5.36
08-24-2011	1710	29	35	8.96	.422	58	.056	1.79	.349	8.41	1.94	5.18
09-27-2011	1740	30	37	10.2	.614	60	.041	1.96	.454	9.13	2.02	5.08
03-14-2012	1510	52	64	15.5	.81	67	.075	2.92	.587	13.3	2.81	7.87
06-19-2012	1350	24	29	8.29	.49	44	.082	1.51	.354	6.66	1.76	4.90

Table 6. Dissolved trace-element concentrations in water samples collected at USGS streamflow-gaging station 15298040, Chulitna River 5 miles above mouth, near Port Alsworth, Alaska, March 2010–June 2012.

[Number in parentheses below constituent is number used by both U.S. Environmental Protection Agency and U.S. Geological Survey to identify parameters in computerized databases. Location of Site No. is shown in figure 3. All values in micrograms per liter. **Abbreviations:** E,estimated; <, less than]

Site 5 – Chulitna River 5 miles above mouth, near Port Alsworth (15298040)

Date	Time	Aluminum (01106)	Antimony (01095)	Arsenic (01000)	Barium (01005)	Beryllium (01010)
03-23-2010	1810	E2 9	0.09	1.21	7.08	<0.012
05-25-2010	1530	18 3	.19	1.56	4.25	<.012
07-21-2010	1720	17 1	.145	1.27	4.24	<.012
08-18-2010	1450	45.0	.099	1.21	3.79	E.006
09-29-2010	1230	12 2	.174	1.33	4.20	<.012
03-09-2011	1740	3.8	.116	1.02	5.47	<.006
05-26-2011	1740	17 9	.143	.943	4.28	<.006
07-13-2011	1320	19.6	.108	1.25	4.21	<.006
08-24-2011	1710	16.1	.096	1.59	3.87	<.006
09-27-2011	1740	12.6	.084	1.68	4.52	<.006
03-14-2012	1510	4.4	.085	1.31	6.46	<.006
06-19-2012	1350	9.9	.129	1.16	3.67	<.006

Boron (01020)	Cadmium (01025)	Chromium (01030)	Cobalt (01035)	Copper (01040)	Iron (01046)	Lead (01049)
3.95	<0.02	E0.067	0.806	<1.0	257	0.122
E2.72	E.013	E.104	1.040	E.92	356	.0699
2.94	<.02	E.101	.268	E.87	151	.0677
2.98	<.02	.154	.157	E.70	200	.0449
E2.73	<.02	.121	1.690	E.64	263	.0504
3.68	<.016	.090	.534	<.50	212	.0239
<3	<.016	.072	.798	.51	176	.0716
<3	<.016	.137	.200	.55	162	.0595
<3	<.016	.116	.334	.56	241	.0380
<3	<.016	.099	1.480	<.50	363	.0432
3.83	<.016	.303	.072	<.80	310	.0251
3.40	<.016	.076	.402	<.80	125	.1315

Lithium (01130)	Manganese (01056)	Molybdenum (01060)	Nickel (01065)	Selenium (01145)	Silver (01075)	Strontium (01080)
1.30	36.7	0.375	0.239	0.152	<0.010	76.4
.571	14 2	.304	.471	.0688	<.010	39.4
.577	15 3	.280	.266	.0800	<.010	52.4
.656	11.0	.277	.302	.0947	E.006	43.2
.600	26.2	.316	.641	.0898	<.010	56.2
.942	30.2	.343	.509	.1454	<.005	72.5
.573	10.0	.319	.497	.1132	<.005	44.9
.665	12.7	.356	.241	.1173	<.005	50.0
.690	12.7	.341	.337	.1017	<.005	57 1
.841	22.7	.357	.402	.0897	<.005	57.4
.944	62.1	.394	.202	.1211	<.005	78 5
.592	10 3	.353	.242	.1207	<.005	47.4

Thallium (01057)	Uranium (22703)	Vanadium (01085)	Zinc (01090)
<0.020	0.0293	E0.139	<2.8
<.020	.0221	.521	<2.8
<.020	.0234	.314	<2.8
<.020	.0266	.360	<2.8
<.020	.0257	.238	<2.8
<.010	.0233	.156	<1.4
<.010	.0170	.307	<1.4
<.010	.0223	.266	<1.4
<.010	.0235	.272	<1.4
<.010	.0257	.279	<1.4
.066	.0287	.162	<1.4
<.010	.0216	.220	<1.4

Table 7. Concentrations of nutrients, dissolved organic carbon, and suspended sediment in water samples collected at USGS streamflow-gaging station 15298040, Chulitna River 5 miles above mouth, near Port Alsworth, Alaska, March 2010–June 2012.

[Number in parentheses below constituent is number used by both U.S. Environmental Protection Agency and U.S. Geological Survey to identify parameters in computerized databases. All values in milligrams per liter unless otherwise noted. **Abbreviations:** mm, millimeter; E, estimated; <, less than; –, constituent not measured]

Date	Time	Dissolved ammonia nitrogen (NH₄) (00608)	Dissolved nitrogen (NH₄+Org) (00623)	Total nitrogen (NH₄+Org) (00625)	Dissolved nitrogen (NO₂+NO₃) (00631)	Dissolved nitrogen (NO₂) (00613)	Dissolved phos-phorus (P) (00666)	Dissolved phos-phorus ortho (PO₄) (00671)	Total phos-phorus (P) (00665)	Dissolved organic carbon (DOC) (00681)	Sus-pended sediment (80154)	Percent finer than 0.0625 (mm) (70331)
					Site 5 – Chulitna River 5 miles above mouth, near Port Alsworth (15298040)							
03-23-2010	1810	E0.016	0.101	E0.085	0.179	<0.002	E0.0037	0.0086	0.0088	1.01	2	86
05-25-2010	1530	<.020	.173	.234	.0958	<.002	.0070	E.0054	.0243	3.53	12	90
07-21-2010	1720	<.020	.165	.266	.0968	E.0017	<.006	E.0072	.0288	4.25	22	87
08-18-2010	1450	<.020	.175	.227	.0699	E.0012	E.0048	E.0058	.0298	5.26	21	70
09-29-2010	1230	<.020	.175	.249	.0749	<.002	E.0047	E.0063	.0222	3.25	9	95
03-09-2011	1740	.015	.092	.057	.175	<.001	.0064	.00566	.0074	1.18	2	92
05-26-2011	1740	<.010	.085	.188	.176	<.001	.0046	<.004	.0276	2.19	20	86
07-13-2011	1320	<.010	.117	.196	.067	.001	.0032	.00587	.0139	3.72	9	95
08-24-2011	1710	<.010	.150	.213	.056	<.001	.0043	<.004	.0146	4.45	6	79
09-27-2011	1740	.011	.167	.166	.044	<.001	.0047	.00467	.0142	3.71	4	87
03-14-2012	1510	.019	.104	E.072	.165	.001	.0099	.00683	E.0128	1.59	2	90
06-19-2012	1350	.014	.098	.129	.117	<.001	<.0030	<.004	.0137	2.42	9	–

Table 8. Results from a blank sample collected at USGS streamflow-gaging station 15298040, Chulitna River 5 miles above mouth, near Port Alsworth, Alaska, August 18, 2010.

[Number in parentheses below constituent is number used by both U.S. Environmental Protection Agency and U.S. Geological Survey to identify parameters in computerized databases. All values in milligrams per liter unless otherwise noted. **Abbreviations:** μg/L, microgram per liter; E, estimated; <, less than]

Date	Time	Alkalinity (39086)	Calcium (00915)	Chloride (00940)	Dissolved solids (70300)	Fluoride (00950)	Magnesium (00925)	Potassium (00935)	Silica (00955)	Sodium (00930)	Sulfate (00945)
08-18-2010	1458	<8.0	<0.044	E0.08	<10	<0.08	<0.016	<0.06	<0.058	<0.10	<0.18

Dissolved ammonia nitrogen (NH₄) (00608)	Dissolved nitrogen (NH₄+Org) (00623)	Total nitrogen (NH₄ + Org) (00625)	Dissolved nitrogen (NO₂+NO₃) (00631)	Dissolved nitrogen (NO₂) (00613)	Dissolved phosphorus (P) (00666)	Phosphorus ortho (PO₄) (00671)	Total phosphorus (P) (00665)	Dissolved organic carbon (DOC) (00681)	Aluminum (01106) (μg/L)	Antimony (01095) (μg/L)	Arsenic (01000) (μg/L)
<0.020	<0.10	<0.10	<0.016	<0.002	<0.006	<0.008	<0.008	<0.66	<3.4	E0.04	<0.04

Barium (01005) (μg/L)	Beryllium (01010) (μg/L)	Boron (01020) (μg/L)	Cadmium (01025) (μg/L)	Chromium (01080) (μg/L)	Cobalt (01035) (μg/L)	Copper (01040) (μg/L)	Iron (10146) (μg/L)	Lead (01049) (μg/L)	Lithium (01130) (μg/L)	Manganese (01056) (μg/L)	Molyb-denum (01060) (μg/L)
<0.14	<0.012	<3	<0.020	<0.12	0.109	<1.0	<6.0	<0.030	<0.44	E0.23	<0.028

Nickel (01065) (μg/L)	Selenium (01145) (μg/L)	Silver (01075) (μg/L)	Strontium (01080) (μg/L)	Thallium (01057) (μg/L)	Uranium (22703) (μg/L)	Vanadium (01085) (μg/L)	Zinc (01090) (μg/L)
<0.12	<0.04	<0.010	<0.40	<0.020	<0.008	<0.16	<2.8

Table 9.   Results from a replicate sample collected at USGS streamflow-gaging station 15298040, Chulitna River 5 miles above mouth, near Port Alsworth, Alaska, March 9, 2011.

[Number in parentheses below constituent is number used by both U.S. Environmental Protection Agency and U.S. Geological Survey to identify parameters in computerized databases. **Abbreviations:** mg/L, milligram per liter; µg/L, microgram per liter; E, estimated; <, less than]

	Date	Time	Calcium (mg/L) (00915)	Chloride (mg/L) (00940)	Dissolved solids (mg/L) (70300)	Fluoride (mg/L) (00950)	Mag-nesium (mg/L) (00925)	Potassium (mg/L) (00935)	Silica (mg/L) (00955)	Sodium (mg/L) (00930)	Sulfate (mg/L) (00945)
Sample	03-09-11	1740	15.3	0.71	66	0.06	2.65	0.63	11.8	2.72	8.80
Replicate	03-09-11	1750	15.1	.71	69	.08	2.62	.58	11.8	2.71	8.87

	Dissolved ammonia nitrogen (NH$_4$) (mg/L) (00608)	Dissolved nitrogen (NH$_4$+Org) (mg/L) (00623)	Total nitrogen (NH$_4$ + Org) (mg/L) (00625)	Dissolved nitrogen (NO$_2$+NO$_3$) (mg/L) (00631)	Dissolved nitrogen (NO$_2$) (mg/L) (00613)	Dissolved phos-phorus (P) (mg/L) (00666)	Phos-phorus Ortho (PO$_4$) (mg/L) (00671)	Total phos-phorus (P) (mg/L) (00665)	Dissolved organic carbon (DOC) (mg/L) (00681)	Aluminum (µg/L) (01106)	Antimony (µg/L) (01095)
Sample	0.015	0.09	0.06	0.175	<0.001	0.006	0.006	0.007	1.18	3.8	0.116
Replicate	.016	.06	.23	.180	<.001	.010	.006	.008	1.45	3.4	.129

	Arsenic (µg/L) (01000)	Barium (µg/L) (01005)	Beryllium (µg/L) (01010)	Boron (µg/L) (01020)	Cadmium (µg/L) (01025)	Chromium (µg/L) (01030)	Cobalt (µg/L) (01035)	Copper (µg/L) (01040)	Iron (µg/L) (01046)	Lead (µg/L) (01049)	Lithium (µg/L) (01130)
Sample	1.0	5.47	<0.006	4	<0.016	0.09	0.534	<0.50	212	0.024	0.94
Replicate	1.0	5.55	<.006	4	<.016	.09	.849	<.50	204	.024	.96

	Man-ganese (µg/L) (01056)	Molyb-denum (µg/L) (01060)	Nickel (µg/L) (01065)	Selenium (µg/L) (01145)	Silver (µg/L) (01075)	Strontium (µg/L) (01080)	Thallium (µg/L) (01057)	Uranium (µg/L) (22703)	Vanadium (µg/L) (01085)	Zinc (µg/L) (01090)	
Sample	30.2	0.343	0.51	0.15	0.005	72.5	<0.010	0.023	0.16	<1.4	
Replicate	30.8	.346	.53	.14	.005	72.3	<.010	.022	.14	<1.4	

Table 10. Water temperature data for USGS streamflow-gaging station 15298040, Chulitna River 5 miles above mouth, near Port Alsworth, Alaska, water years 2010 and 2011.

[**Abbreviations:** Max, maximum; Min, minimum; –, no data]

Day	Temperature, water, degrees Celsius, water year October 2009 to September 2010											
---	October			November			December			January		
	Max	Min	Mean	Max	Min	Mean	Max	Min	Mean	Max	Min	Mean
1	–	–	–	0.0	0.0	0.0	0.0	0.0	0.0	0.0	0.0	0.0
2	–	–	–	0.0	0.0	0.0	0.0	0.0	0.0	0.0	0.0	0.0
3	–	–	–	0.0	0.0	0.0	0.0	0.0	0.0	0.0	0.0	0.0
4	–	–	–	0.0	0.0	0.0	0.0	0.0	0.0	0.0	0.0	0.0
5	–	–	–	0.0	0.0	0.0	0.0	0.0	0.0	0.0	0.0	0.0
6	–	–	–	0.0	0.0	0.0	0.0	0.0	0.0	0.0	0.0	0.0
7	–	–	–	0.0	0.0	0.0	0.0	0.0	0.0	0.0	0.0	0.0
8	7.0	6.0	6.5	0.0	0.0	0.0	0.0	0.0	0.0	0.0	0.0	0.0
9	8.0	7.0	7.5	0.0	0.0	0.0	0.0	0.0	0.0	0.0	0.0	0.0
10	8.5	8.0	8.5	0.0	0.0	0.0	0.0	0.0	0.0	0.0	0.0	0.0
11	8.0	7.5	8.0	0.0	0.0	0.0	0.0	0.0	0.0	0.0	0.0	0.0
12	8.5	8.0	8.0	0.0	0.0	0.0	0.0	0.0	0.0	0.0	0.0	0.0
13	8.5	8.0	8.0	0.0	0.0	0.0	0.0	0.0	0.0	0.0	0.0	0.0
14	8.0	7.5	7.5	0.0	0.0	0.0	0.0	0.0	0.0	0.0	0.0	0.0
15	7.5	6.0	6.5	0.0	0.0	0.0	0.0	0.0	0.0	0.0	0.0	0.0
16	6.0	5.0	5.5	0.0	0.0	0.0	0.0	0.0	0.0	0.0	0.0	0.0
17	5.5	4.5	4.5	0.0	0.0	0.0	0.0	0.0	0.0	0.0	0.0	0.0
18	4.5	4.0	4.0	0.0	0.0	0.0	0.0	0.0	0.0	0.0	0.0	0.0
19	4.0	3.5	4.0	0.0	0.0	0.0	0.0	0.0	0.0	0.0	0.0	0.0
20	4.0	3.5	4.0	0.0	0.0	0.0	0.0	0.0	0.0	0.0	0.0	0.0
21	4.0	3.0	3.5	0.0	0.0	0.0	0.0	0.0	0.0	0.0	0.0	0.0
22	3.0	2.5	2.5	0.0	0.0	0.0	0.0	0.0	0.0	0.0	0.0	0.0
23	3.0	2.5	2.5	0.0	0.0	0.0	0.0	0.0	0.0	0.0	0.0	0.0
24	3.5	3.0	3.5	0.0	0.0	0.0	0.0	0.0	0.0	0.0	0.0	0.0
25	3.5	3.0	3.0	0.0	0.0	0.0	0.0	0.0	0.0	0.0	0.0	0.0
26	3.0	2.0	2.5	0.0	0.0	0.0	0.0	0.0	0.0	0.0	0.0	0.0
27	2.0	1.0	1.5	0.0	0.0	0.0	0.0	0.0	0.0	0.0	0.0	0.0
28	1.0	0.0	0.0	0.0	0.0	0.0	0.0	0.0	0.0	0.0	0.0	0.0
29	0.0	0.0	0.0	0.0	0.0	0.0	0.0	0.0	0.0	0.0	0.0	0.0
30	0.0	0.0	0.0	0.0	0.0	0.0	0.0	0.0	0.0	0.0	0.0	0.0
31	0.0	0.0	0.0	–	–	–	0.0	0.0	0.0	0.0	0.0	0.0
Month	–	–	–	0.0	0.0	0.0	0.0	0.0	0.0	0.0	0.0	0.0

Table 10.   Water temperature data for USGS streamflow-gaging station 15298040, Chulitna River 5 miles above mouth, near Port Alsworth, Alaska, water years 2010 and 2011.—Continued

[**Abbreviations:** Max, maximum; Min, minimum; –, no data]

Day	Temperature, water, degrees Celsius, water year October 2009 to September 2010											
---	February			March			April			May		
	Max	Min	Mean	Max	Min	Mean	Max	Min	Mean	Max	Min	Mean
1	0.0	0.0	0.0	0.0	0.0	0.0	0.0	0.0	0.0	0.0	0.0	0.0
2	0.0	0.0	0.0	0.0	0.0	0.0	0.0	0.0	0.0	0.0	0.0	0.0
3	0.0	0.0	0.0	0.0	0.0	0.0	0.0	0.0	0.0	0.5	0.0	0.0
4	0.0	0.0	0.0	0.0	0.0	0.0	0.0	0.0	0.0	0.5	0.0	0.0
5	0.0	0.0	0.0	0.0	0.0	0.0	0.0	0.0	0.0	3.0	0.0	0.5
6	0.0	0.0	0.0	0.0	0.0	0.0	0.0	0.0	0.0	3.0	1.5	2.0
7	0.0	0.0	0.0	0.0	0.0	0.0	0.0	0.0	0.0	3.5	1.5	2.5
8	0.0	0.0	0.0	0.0	0.0	0.0	0.0	0.0	0.0	4.0	1.5	2.5
9	0.0	0.0	0.0	0.0	0.0	0.0	0.0	0.0	0.0	4.5	2.5	3.0
10	0.0	0.0	0.0	0.0	0.0	0.0	0.0	0.0	0.0	4.0	2.5	3.0
11	0.0	0.0	0.0	0.0	0.0	0.0	0.0	0.0	0.0	4.0	2.5	3.0
12	0.0	0.0	0.0	0.0	0.0	0.0	0.0	0.0	0.0	3.0	2.5	3.0
13	0.0	0.0	0.0	0.0	0.0	0.0	0.0	0.0	0.0	3.5	2.0	3.0
14	0.0	0.0	0.0	0.0	0.0	0.0	0.0	0.0	0.0	3.5	2.5	3.0
15	0.0	0.0	0.0	0.0	0.0	0.0	0.0	0.0	0.0	6.0	3.5	4.5
16	0.0	0.0	0.0	0.0	0.0	0.0	0.0	0.0	0.0	6.5	5.0	5.5
17	0.0	0.0	0.0	0.0	0.0	0.0	0.0	0.0	0.0	7.0	5.0	6.0
18	0.0	0.0	0.0	0.0	0.0	0.0	0.0	0.0	0.0	7.0	5.0	6.0
19	0.0	0.0	0.0	0.0	0.0	0.0	0.0	0.0	0.0	7.5	6.0	7.0
20	0.0	0.0	0.0	0.0	0.0	0.0	0.0	0.0	0.0	8.5	7.0	7.5
21	0.0	0.0	0.0	0.0	0.0	0.0	0.0	0.0	0.0	8.5	6.0	7.5
22	0.0	0.0	0.0	0.0	0.0	0.0	0.0	0.0	0.0	8.5	7.5	7.5
23	0.0	0.0	0.0	0.0	0.0	0.0	0.0	0.0	0.0	8.0	6.5	7.5
24	0.0	0.0	0.0	0.0	0.0	0.0	0.0	0.0	0.0	8.0	7.0	7.5
25	0.0	0.0	0.0	0.0	0.0	0.0	0.0	0.0	0.0	10.0	7.0	8.0
26	0.0	0.0	0.0	0.0	0.0	0.0	0.0	0.0	0.0	12.0	8.5	10.0
27	0.0	0.0	0.0	0.0	0.0	0.0	0.0	0.0	0.0	13.0	10.0	11.0
28	0.0	0.0	0.0	0.0	0.0	0.0	0.0	0.0	0.0	12.5	10.5	11.0
29	–	–	–	0.0	0.0	0.0	0.0	0.0	0.0	13.0	10.0	11.5
30	–	–	–	0.0	0.0	0.0	0.0	0.0	0.0	13.5	11.5	12.5
31	–	–	–	0.0	0.0	0.0	–	–	–	13.5	11.5	12.5
Month	0.0	0.0	0.0	0.0	0.0	0.0	0.0	0.0	0.0	13.5	0.0	5.4

Table 10.   Water temperature data for USGS streamflow-gaging station 15298040, Chulitna River 5 miles above mouth, near Port Alsworth, Alaska, water years 2010 and 2011.—Continued

[**Abbreviations:** Max, maximum; Min, minimum; –, no data]

Day	Temperature, water, degrees Celsius, water year October 2009 to September 2010											
	June			July			August			September		
	Max	Min	Mean	Max	Min	Mean	Max	Min	Mean	Max	Min	Mean
1	14.0	11.5	12.5	14.5	12.5	13.0	11.0	10.0	10.5	11.5	10.5	11.0
2	13.5	12.0	12.5	12.5	11.0	12.0	13.5	10.5	11.5	11.0	10.0	10.5
3	12.5	10.5	11.5	13.0	11.5	12.0	13.5	12.0	12.5	11.0	9.5	10.5
4	10.5	9.5	10.0	13.0	12.0	12.5	12.5	12.0	12.0	11.0	10.5	10.5
5	10.0	7.5	9.0	12.5	11.5	12.0	12.5	11.5	12.0	11.0	10.0	10.5
6	11.0	9.0	10.0	11.5	10.5	10.5	12.0	11.0	11.5	11.0	10.0	10.5
7	11.5	10.0	10.5	10.5	10.0	10.0	11.0	10.0	10.5	11.0	10.5	11.0
8	12.5	10.0	11.5	12.5	9.5	11.0	10.0	10.0	10.0	10.5	10.0	10.5
9	12.5	10.5	11.0	12.5	11.0	12.0	10.0	10.0	10.0	10.0	9.5	10.0
10	11.5	10.0	10.5	12.0	11.5	12.0	10.0	9.5	10.0	10.5	9.0	9.5
11	12.5	9.5	11.0	12.0	11.0	11.5	10.0	9.0	9.5	10.5	9.0	9.5
12	13.0	11.0	12.0	14.5	11.5	12.5	9.0	8.5	9.0	10.5	9.0	10.0
13	14.0	11.5	12.5	14.5	13.0	13.5	10.0	9.0	9.5	11.0	9.5	10.0
14	13.5	11.5	12.5	14.0	12.5	13.0	12.0	10.0	10.5	11.0	9.5	10.0
15	11.5	9.5	10.5	14.0	12.5	13.0	12.0	11.5	11.5	11.0	9.0	10.0
16	10.0	9.0	9.5	15.0	12.0	13.5	11.5	10.5	10.5	11.0	9.5	10.0
17	10.5	9.0	9.5	16.0	13.5	14.5	10.5	10.0	10.5	10.5	9.5	10.0
18	11.0	9.5	10.0	16.0	14.5	15.0	10.0	9.5	10.0	10.0	9.0	9.5
19	12.5	10.0	11.0	14.5	12.5	13.5	10.5	9.0	9.5	10.0	8.5	9.5
20	13.5	10.5	12.0	12.5	11.0	12.0	11.0	9.5	10.0	10.0	8.5	9.0
21	15.0	12.0	13.0	11.5	10.0	11.0	11.0	10.0	10.5	9.5	8.5	9.0
22	15.5	13.5	14.5	12.5	10.5	11.5	12.0	10.5	11.0	9.5	8.5	9.0
23	17.0	14.5	15.5	12.0	10.0	11.0	12.5	10.5	11.5	8.5	7.5	8.0
24	16.5	14.5	15.5	10.0	9.0	9.5	13.5	11.5	12.5	8.0	6.5	7.0
25	15.5	13.5	14.5	9.0	9.0	9.0	13.5	12.0	12.5	7.0	5.5	6.0
26	15.0	13.5	14.5	9.5	8.5	9.0	13.5	12.5	13.0	5.5	4.0	4.5
27	15.0	13.5	14.0	10.0	9.0	9.5	13.0	12.5	12.5	4.0	2.5	3.0
28	15.0	12.5	13.5	10.0	9.5	9.5	12.5	11.5	11.5	3.0	2.0	2.5
29	14.5	13.5	14.0	10.0	9.0	9.5	12.0	10.5	11.5	4.0	2.5	3.5
30	15.0	12.5	13.5	9.5	9.0	9.0	12.0	11.0	11.5	5.0	4.0	4.5
31	–	–	–	10.0	9.5	9.5	12.0	11.0	11.5	–	–	–
Month	17.0	7.5	12.1	16.0	8.5	11.5	13.5	8.5	11.0	11.5	2.0	8.6

Table 10. Water temperature data for USGS streamflow-gaging station 15298040, Chulitna River 5 miles above mouth, near Port Alsworth, Alaska, water years 2010 and 2011.—Continued

[**Abbreviations:** Max, maximum; Min, minimum; –, no data]

Day	\multicolumn{12}{c}{Temperature, water, degrees Celsius, water year October 2010 to September 2011}
	\multicolumn{3}{c}{October}	\multicolumn{3}{c}{November}	\multicolumn{3}{c}{December}	\multicolumn{3}{c}{January}
	Max	Min	Mean	Max	Min	Mean	Max	Min	Mean	Max	Min	Mean
1	6.0	5.0	5.5	0.0	0.0	0.0	0.0	0.0	0.0	0.0	0.0	0.0
2	5.5	5.5	5.5	0.0	0.0	0.0	0.0	0.0	0.0	0.0	0.0	0.0
3	5.5	4.0	5.0	0.0	0.0	0.0	0.0	0.0	0.0	0.0	0.0	0.0
4	4.0	3.5	3.5	0.0	0.0	0.0	0.0	0.0	0.0	0.0	0.0	0.0
5	4.0	3.0	3.5	0.0	0.0	0.0	0.0	0.0	0.0	0.0	0.0	0.0
6	3.5	2.0	3.0	0.0	0.0	0.0	0.0	0.0	0.0	0.0	0.0	0.0
7	3.0	2.0	2.5	0.0	0.0	0.0	0.0	0.0	0.0	0.0	0.0	0.0
8	2.5	1.5	2.0	0.0	0.0	0.0	0.0	0.0	0.0	0.0	0.0	0.0
9	2.5	2.0	2.0	0.0	0.0	0.0	0.0	0.0	0.0	0.0	0.0	0.0
10	2.0	1.5	2.0	0.0	0.0	0.0	0.0	0.0	0.0	0.0	0.0	0.0
11	2.0	1.5	2.0	0.0	0.0	0.0	0.0	0.0	0.0	0.0	0.0	0.0
12	2.0	1.0	1.5	0.0	0.0	0.0	0.0	0.0	0.0	–	–	–
13	1.5	0.5	1.0	0.0	0.0	0.0	0.0	0.0	0.0	–	–	–
14	1.0	0.0	0.0	0.0	0.0	0.0	0.0	0.0	0.0	–	–	–
15	0.5	0.0	0.0	0.0	0.0	0.0	0.0	0.0	0.0	–	–	–
16	1.0	0.0	0.5	0.0	0.0	0.0	0.0	0.0	0.0	–	–	–
17	2.0	1.0	1.5	0.0	0.0	0.0	0.0	0.0	0.0	–	–	–
18	2.0	2.0	2.0	0.0	0.0	0.0	0.0	0.0	0.0	–	–	–
19	2.0	1.5	1.5	0.0	0.0	0.0	0.0	0.0	0.0	–	–	–
20	2.0	1.5	1.5	0.0	0.0	0.0	0.0	0.0	0.0	–	–	–
21	2.5	2.0	2.0	0.0	0.0	0.0	0.0	0.0	0.0	–	–	–
22	3.0	2.0	2.5	0.0	0.0	0.0	0.0	0.0	0.0	–	–	–
23	3.0	2.5	2.5	0.0	0.0	0.0	0.0	0.0	0.0	–	–	–
24	2.5	2.5	2.5	0.0	0.0	0.0	0.0	0.0	0.0	–	–	–
25	2.5	1.5	2.0	0.0	0.0	0.0	0.0	0.0	0.0	–	–	–
26	1.5	1.5	1.5	0.0	0.0	0.0	0.0	0.0	0.0	–	–	–
27	1.5	0.0	0.5	0.0	0.0	0.0	0.0	0.0	0.0	–	–	–
28	1.0	1.0	1.0	0.0	0.0	0.0	0.0	0.0	0.0	–	–	–
29	1.0	1.0	1.0	0.0	0.0	0.0	0.0	0.0	0.0	–	–	–
30	1.0	0.0	0.5	0.0	0.0	0.0	0.0	0.0	0.0	–	–	–
31	0.0	0.0	0.0	–	–	–	0.0	0.0	0.0	–	–	–
Month	6.0	0.0	2.0	0.0	0.0	0.0	0.0	0.0	0.0	–	–	–

Table 10.   Water temperature data for USGS streamflow-gaging station 15298040, Chulitna River 5 miles above mouth, near Port Alsworth, Alaska, water years 2010 and 2011.—Continued

[**Abbreviations:** Max, maximum; Min, minimum; –, no data]

Day	Temperature, water, degrees Celsius, water year October 2010 to September 2011											
	February			March			April			May		
	Max	Min	Mean	Max	Min	Mean	Max	Min	Mean	Max	Min	Mean
1	–	–	–	–	–	–	0.0	0.0	0.0	0.0	0.0	0.0
2	–	–	–	–	–	–	0.0	0.0	0.0	2.0	0.0	0.5
3	–	–	–	–	–	–	0.0	0.0	0.0	3.0	1.0	2.0
4	–	–	–	–	–	–	0.0	0.0	0.0	3.5	1.5	2.5
5	–	–	–	–	–	–	0.0	0.0	0.0	3.5	1.5	2.5
6	–	–	–	–	–	–	0.0	0.0	0.0	4.5	1.5	3.0
7	–	–	–	–	–	–	0.0	0.0	0.0	4.0	2.0	3.0
8	–	–	–	–	–	–	0.0	0.0	0.0	3.5	2.5	3.0
9	–	–	–	0.0	0.0	0.0	0.0	0.0	0.0	4.0	2.5	3.0
10	–	–	–	0.0	0.0	0.0	0.0	0.0	0.0	5.5	2.5	3.5
11	–	–	–	0.0	0.0	0.0	0.0	0.0	0.0	6.0	3.5	4.5
12	–	–	–	0.0	0.0	0.0	0.0	0.0	0.0	6.0	3.0	4.5
13	–	–	–	0.0	0.0	0.0	0.0	0.0	0.0	7.5	4.0	5.5
14	–	–	–	0.0	0.0	0.0	0.0	0.0	0.0	7.0	6.0	6.0
15	–	–	–	0.0	0.0	0.0	0.0	0.0	0.0	6.0	5.0	5.5
16	–	–	–	0.0	0.0	0.0	0.0	0.0	0.0	6.0	5.0	5.5
17	–	–	–	0.0	0.0	0.0	0.0	0.0	0.0	6.0	5.0	5.5
18	–	–	–	0.0	0.0	0.0	0.0	0.0	0.0	7.0	5.0	6.0
19	–	–	–	0.0	0.0	0.0	0.0	0.0	0.0	7.0	6.5	7.0
20	–	–	–	0.0	0.0	0.0	0.0	0.0	0.0	7.0	5.5	6.0
21	–	–	–	0.0	0.0	0.0	0.0	0.0	0.0	8.0	6.0	7.0
22	–	–	–	0.0	0.0	0.0	0.0	0.0	0.0	8.5	6.5	7.5
23	–	–	–	0.0	0.0	0.0	0.0	0.0	0.0	8.5	7.0	7.5
24	–	–	–	0.0	0.0	0.0	0.0	0.0	0.0	7.5	6.5	7.0
25	–	–	–	0.0	0.0	0.0	0.0	0.0	0.0	8.5	5.5	7.0
26	–	–	–	0.0	0.0	0.0	0.0	0.0	0.0	8.5	7.5	8.0
27	–	–	–	0.0	0.0	0.0	0.0	0.0	0.0	10.0	7.5	8.5
28	–	–	–	0.0	0.0	0.0	0.0	0.0	0.0	10.0	9.0	9.5
29	–	–	–	0.0	0.0	0.0	0.0	0.0	0.0	9.5	8.5	9.0
30	–	–	–	0.0	0.0	0.0	0.0	0.0	0.0	11.0	8.5	9.5
31	–	–	–	0.0	0.0	0.0	–	–	–	11.0	9.5	10.0
Month	–	–	–	–	–	–	0.0	0.0	0.0	11.0	0.0	5.5

Table 10.   Water temperature data for USGS streamflow-gaging station 15298040, Chulitna River 5 miles above mouth, near Port Alsworth, Alaska, water years 2010 and 2011.—Continued

[**Abbreviations:** Max, maximum; Min, minimum; –, no data]

Day	Temperature, water, degrees Celsius, water year October 2010 to September 2011											
	June			July			August			September		
	Max	Min	Mean	Max	Min	Mean	Max	Min	Mean	Max	Min	Mean
1	9.5	7.5	8.5	13.5	11.0	12.0	13.5	12.5	12.5	10.5	9.5	10.0
2	10.5	7.0	8.0	13.5	12.0	12.5	12.5	11.5	11.5	10.5	10.0	10.0
3	10.0	8.5	9.0	12.5	12.0	12.0	11.5	10.5	11.0	10.5	10.0	10.0
4	8.5	7.5	8.0	12.0	11.0	11.5	11.5	10.5	11.0	10.5	9.5	10.0
5	9.5	7.0	8.0	13.5	10.5	11.5	10.5	9.5	10.0	10.5	9.0	9.5
6	9.0	7.5	8.5	14.5	12.5	13.0	10.5	9.0	9.5	10.0	8.5	9.0
7	9.0	8.0	8.5	14.0	12.5	13.0	10.5	8.5	9.5	10.0	9.0	9.5
8	9.5	7.5	8.5	12.5	11.0	11.5	10.0	9.5	9.5	10.0	9.5	9.5
9	10.0	8.5	9.0	12.0	11.0	11.5	10.0	8.5	9.0	10.0	8.0	9.0
10	11.0	9.0	10.0	11.5	10.5	11.0	11.0	9.5	10.0	9.5	9.0	9.5
11	11.0	10.0	10.5	11.0	10.5	10.5	12.0	10.0	11.0	10.5	9.0	10.0
12	11.0	10.0	10.5	11.0	10.5	10.5	11.5	11.0	11.5	10.0	9.0	9.5
13	10.5	10.0	10.5	11.5	10.0	10.5	12.0	11.0	11.5	9.5	9.0	9.5
14	10.5	9.5	10.0	12.0	10.5	11.0	12.5	12.0	12.0	9.5	9.0	9.0
15	11.0	8.5	9.5	14.0	11.0	12.0	12.5	11.0	12.0	9.5	8.5	9.0
16	13.0	9.5	11.0	15.0	12.5	13.5	13.0	11.0	12.0	9.0	8.0	9.0
17	13.5	11.0	12.5	15.0	12.0	13.0	13.5	12.0	13.0	9.0	8.0	8.5
18	14.5	12.0	13.0	12.5	11.0	11.5	13.0	12.0	12.5	9.0	8.0	8.5
19	14.0	12.0	13.0	14.5	11.0	12.5	13.0	11.5	12.0	8.5	7.5	8.0
20	12.0	9.5	11.0	15.0	13.0	14.0	12.0	11.0	11.5	8.5	7.5	8.0
21	9.5	8.0	8.5	14.5	13.5	14.0	12.0	11.0	11.5	9.0	8.0	8.5
22	9.0	8.0	8.0	16.0	13.0	14.5	12.0	11.0	11.0	9.0	8.0	8.5
23	11.0	8.0	9.0	16.0	13.5	14.5	11.5	10.0	11.0	8.5	7.5	8.0
24	12.0	10.0	11.0	13.5	11.5	12.0	11.0	10.0	10.5	8.5	7.5	7.5
25	12.0	10.5	11.0	12.0	10.5	11.0	11.0	10.0	10.5	8.0	6.5	7.5
26	11.5	9.5	10.5	12.5	11.0	12.0	12.0	10.0	11.0	8.0	6.5	7.0
27	11.5	10.5	11.0	13.5	11.5	12.5	11.5	10.0	10.5	7.5	6.5	7.0
28	10.5	9.5	10.0	14.5	12.0	13.0	12.5	10.5	11.0	7.0	5.5	6.0
29	10.5	9.0	10.0	14.0	13.0	13.5	12.0	10.5	11.5	6.5	5.5	6.0
30	12.0	10.0	11.0	14.5	13.0	13.5	12.5	11.5	12.0	5.5	4.0	4.5
31	–	–	–	14.5	13.0	13.5	12.0	10.5	11.0	–	–	–
Month	14.5	7.0	9.9	16.0	10.0	12.3	13.5	8.5	11.1	10.5	4.0	8.5

Table 11.   Dissolved oxygen data for USGS streamflow-gaging station 15298040, Chulitna River 5 miles above mouth, near Port Alsworth, Alaska, water years 2010 and 2011.

[**Abbreviations:** Max, maximum; Min, minimum; –, no data]

Day	Dissolved oxygen, water, unfiltered, milligrams per liter, water year October 2009 to September 2010											
---	April		May		June		July		August		September	
	Max	Min	Max	Min	Max	Min	Max	Min	Max	Min	Max	Min
1	–	–	–	–	11.5	10.9	11.3	10.3	11.1	10.9	10.6	10.2
2	–	–	–	–	11.4	10.7	11.4	10.8	11.0	10.6	10.7	10.3
3	–	–	–	–	11.6	10.8	11.4	10.8	10.6	10.3	10.7	10.4
4	–	–	–	–	12.2	11.4	11.2	10.5	10.5	10.2	10.4	10.2
5	–	–	–	–	12.6	12.1	11.3	10.6	10.4	10.2	10.5	10.2
6	–	–	–	–	12.4	11.8	11.8	11.0	10.4	10.1	10.5	10.3
7	–	–	–	–	12.1	11.5	11.8	11.3	10.7	10.3	10.4	10.1
8	–	–	–	–	12.0	11.5	11.9	11.3	10.7	10.6	10.7	10.3
9	–	–	–	–	11.9	11.2	11.5	10.9	10.7	10.5	10.8	10.5
10	–	–	–	–	12.1	11.4	11.3	10.6	10.8	10.5	10.9	10.5
11	–	–	–	–	12.0	11.5	11.4	10.6	11.1	10.7	11.0	10.5
12	–	–	–	–	11.7	11.1	11.2	10.6	11.2	11.0	11.0	10.5
13	–	–	–	–	11.6	10.9	10.8	10.0	11.1	10.8	11.0	10.4
14	–	–	–	–	11.4	10.7	11.1	10.2	10.8	10.4	10.9	10.3
15	–	–	–	–	11.8	11.0	11.1	10.3	10.4	10.1	10.9	10.4
16	–	–	–	–	12.1	11.6	11.3	10.4	10.5	10.3	10.9	10.3
17	–	–	–	–	12.3	11.7	11.1	9.8	10.8	10.3	10.9	10.3
18	–	–	–	–	12.3	11.6	10.6	9.6	10.8	10.6	11.0	10.5
19	–	–	–	–	12.1	11.4	10.8	9.8	11.0	10.7	11.0	10.5
20	–	–	–	–	12.0	11.1	11.0	10.4	10.8	10.5	11.1	10.5
21	–	–	–	–	11.6	10.8	11.7	10.8	10.6	10.3	11.0	10.6
22	–	–	–	–	11.3	10.3	11.6	10.9	10.5	10.3	11.1	10.4
23	–	–	–	–	11.1	10.2	11.3	10.8	10.6	10.2	11.2	10.6
24	–	–	–	–	10.9	9.9	11.7	11.2	10.2	10.0	11.2	10.6
25	–	–	–	–	11.1	10.2	11.8	11.3	10.2	9.9	11.6	10.9
26	–	–	12.5	11.9	11.1	10.2	11.8	11.4	10.0	9.8	12.2	11.3
27	–	–	12.2	11.7	10.9	10.0	11.7	11.4	10.1	9.7	12.7	12.0
28	–	–	12.2	11.5	11.3	10.4	11.5	11.2	10.3	9.9	12.8	12.2
29	–	–	11.9	11.5	11.1	10.2	11.5	11.2	10.4	10.1	–	12.2
30	–	–	11.6	11.1	11.3	10.3	11.4	11.2	10.3	10.1	–	–
31	–	–	11.6	10.8	–	–	11.2	11.0	10.4	10.1	–	–
Month	–	–	–	–	12.6	9.9	11.9	9.6	11.2	9.7	–	–

Table 11.   Dissolved oxygen data for USGS streamflow-gaging station 15298040, Chulitna River 5 miles above mouth, near Port Alsworth, Alaska, water years 2010 and 2011.—Continued

[**Abbreviations:** Max, maximum; Min, minimum; –, no data]

Day	Dissolved oxygen, water, unfiltered, milligrams per liter, water year October 2010 to September 2011											
---	April		May		June		July		August		September	
	Max	Min	Max	Min	Max	Min	Max	Min	Max	Min	Max	Min
1	–	–	–	–	12.1	11.3	11.0	10.6	10.5	10.1	11.4	10.9
2	–	–	–	–	12.2	11.5	10.8	10.3	10.8	10.3	11.1	10.7
3	–	–	–	–	11.8	11.1	11.0	10.3	11.0	10.6	11.1	10.6
4	–	–	–	–	12.3	11.5	11.1	10.5	11.0	10.5	11.2	10.6
5	–	–	–	–	12.3	11.8	11.2	10.7	11.5	10.9	11.0	10.4
6	–	–	–	–	12.3	11.7	10.9	10.3	11.4	11.1	–	–
7	–	–	–	–	12.0	11.5	10.9	10.3	11.7	11.3	11.3	10.5
8	–	–	–	–	12.2	11.7	11.1	10.5	11.4	11.2	11.7	10.8
9	–	–	–	–	12.0	11.4	11.1	10.6	11.6	11.2	12.2	11.2
10	–	–	–	–	11.8	11.2	11.4	10.8	11.4	11.0	–	–
11	–	–	–	–	11.7	10.9	11.3	11.0	11.3	10.7	–	–
12	–	–	–	–	11.6	10.9	11.3	10.8	11.0	10.7	–	–
13	–	–	–	–	11.6	10.9	11.6	11.0	11.0	10.6	–	–
14	–	–	–	–	11.7	10.9	11.5	11.0	10.8	10.2	–	–
15	–	–	–	–	11.8	11.4	11.3	10.8	10.9	10.4	–	–
16	–	–	–	–	11.7	11.0	11.0	10.4	10.9	10.4	–	–
17	–	–	–	–	11.3	10.6	10.8	10.2	10.8	10.2	–	–
18	–	–	–	–	11.1	10.4	11.4	10.8	10.7	10.1	–	–
19	–	–	–	–	11.0	10.2	11.2	10.7	10.4	9.9	–	–
20	–	–	–	–	11.3	10.4	11.0	10.2	10.6	9.8	–	–
21	–	–	–	–	11.9	11.3	10.8	10.1	10.6	9.8	–	–
22	–	–	–	–	11.8	11.5	10.8	10.2	10.7	9.7	–	–
23	–	–	–	–	11.8	11.1	10.4	9.8	11.0	10.3	–	–
24	–	–	–	–	11.2	10.8	11.0	10.2	11.0	10.5	–	–
25	–	–	–	–	11.1	10.7	11.3	10.8	11.1	10.6	–	–
26	–	–	–	–	11.4	10.9	11.1	10.7	11.1	10.6	–	–
27	–	–	12.2	11.6	11.0	10.6	11.1	10.6	11.2	10.5	–	–
28	–	–	11.8	11.2	11.3	10.9	11.1	10.5	11.1	10.6	–	–
29	–	–	12.1	11.4	11.3	11.0	10.8	10.2	11.2	10.5	–	–
30	–	–	12.0	11.4	11.2	10.8	10.8	10.2	11.0	10.4	–	–
31	–	–	11.7	11.0	–	–	10.7	10.0	11.1	10.5	–	–
Month	–	–	–	–	12.3	10.2	11.6	9.8	11.7	9.7	–	–

Table 12. pH data for USGS streamflow-gaging station 15298040, Chulitna River 5 miles above mouth, near Port Alsworth, Alaska, water years 2010 and 2011.

[**Abbreviations:** Max, maximum; Min, minimum; –, no data]

Day	pH, water, unfiltered, field, standard units, water year October 2009 to September 2010											
	April		May		June		July		August		September	
	Max	Min	Max	Min	Max	Min	Max	Min	Max	Min	Max	Min
1	–	–	–	–	7.6	7.4	7.8	7.6	7.3	7.2	7.5	7.4
2	–	–	–	–	7.6	7.5	7.8	7.6	7.4	7.3	7.5	7.4
3	–	–	–	–	7.5	7.5	7.8	7.6	7.4	7.2	7.5	7.4
4	–	–	–	–	7.6	7.5	7.8	7.6	7.3	7.3	7.5	7.4
5	–	–	–	–	7.5	7.4	7.8	7.6	7.3	7.3	7.4	7.3
6	–	–	–	–	7.6	7.5	7.8	7.6	7.3	7.2	7.4	7.3
7	–	–	–	–	7.6	7.5	7.8	7.6	7.3	7.2	7.4	7.3
8	–	–	–	–	7.6	7.5	7.8	7.6	7.3	7.2	7.4	7.3
9	–	–	–	–	7.6	7.4	7.8	7.6	7.3	7.2	7.4	7.3
10	–	–	–	–	7.6	7.5	7.8	7.6	7.4	7.3	7.4	7.4
11	–	–	–	–	7.6	7.5	7.7	7.6	7.3	7.3	7.4	7.4
12	–	–	–	–	7.6	7.5	7.8	7.6	7.3	7.2	7.5	7.4
13	–	–	–	–	7.6	7.5	7.7	7.6	7.3	7.2	7.5	7.4
14	–	–	–	–	7.6	7.5	7.8	7.6	7.3	7.2	7.5	7.4
15	–	–	–	–	7.6	7.4	7.8	7.6	7.3	7.3	7.5	7.4
16	–	–	–	–	7.6	7.4	7.8	7.6	7.3	7.3	7.5	7.4
17	–	–	–	–	7.6	7.5	7.8	7.5	7.4	7.2	7.5	7.4
18	–	–	–	–	7.7	7.5	7.7	7.5	7.3	7.3	7.5	7.4
19	–	–	–	–	7.8	7.6	7.7	7.5	7.4	7.3	7.5	7.4
20	–	–	–	–	7.8	7.6	7.6	7.5	7.4	7.3	7.5	7.4
21	–	–	–	–	7.8	7.6	7.6	7.5	7.4	7.3	7.6	7.5
22	–	–	–	–	7.8	7.6	7.6	7.4	7.4	7.3	7.6	7.5
23	–	–	–	–	7.9	7.6	7.6	7.5	7.4	7.3	7.6	7.5
24	–	–	–	–	7.8	7.6	7.6	7.5	7.4	7.3	7.6	7.5
25	–	–	–	–	7.8	7.6	7.6	7.5	7.4	7.4	7.6	7.5
26	–	–	7.5	7.4	7.8	7.6	7.5	7.4	7.4	7.3	7.6	7.5
27	–	–	7.5	7.4	7.8	7.6	7.4	7.3	7.4	7.4	7.6	7.5
28	–	–	7.5	7.4	7.8	7.6	7.4	7.3	7.5	7.4	7.6	7.5
29	–	–	7.5	7.4	7.8	7.6	7.4	7.3	7.4	7.4	–	7.5
30	–	–	7.5	7.4	7.8	7.6	7.4	7.3	7.5	7.4	–	–
31	–	–	7.5	7.4	–	–	7.3	7.2	7.5	7.4	–	–
Month	–	–	–	–	7.9	7.4	7.8	7.2	7.5	7.2	–	–

Table 12.   pH data for USGS streamflow-gaging station 15298040, Chulitna River 5 miles above mouth, near Port Alsworth, Alaska, water years 2010 and 2011.—Continued

[**Abbreviations:** Max, maximum; Min, minimum; –, no data]

Day	pH, water, unfiltered, field, standard units, water year October 2010 to September 2011											
	April		May		June		July		August		September	
	Max	Min	Max	Min	Max	Min	Max	Min	Max	Min	Max	Min
1	–	–	–	–	7.6	7.5	7.5	7.4	7.4	7.3	7.4	7.3
2	–	–	–	–	7.5	7.4	7.5	7.4	7.4	7.3	7.3	7.1
3	–	–	–	–	7.5	7.4	7.4	7.3	7.4	7.2	7.3	7.2
4	–	–	–	–	7.5	7.5	7.4	7.3	7.3	7.2	7.3	7.2
5	–	–	–	–	7.6	7.5	7.4	7.3	7.4	7.3	7.3	7.2
6	–	–	–	–	7.5	7.4	7.3	7.1	7.3	7.3	7.3	7.2
7	–	–	–	–	7.5	7.4	7.6	7.1	7.4	7.3	7.3	7.2
8	–	–	–	–	7.5	7.4	7.6	7.5	7.3	7.2	7.3	7.2
9	–	–	–	–	7.5	7.4	7.6	7.5	7.3	7.2	7.3	7.2
10	–	–	–	–	7.6	7.4	7.6	7.5	7.3	7.2	7.3	7.1
11	–	–	–	–	7.6	7.4	7.6	7.5	7.4	7.2	7.4	7.2
12	–	–	–	–	7.5	7.4	7.6	7.5	7.4	7.3	7.3	7.2
13	–	–	–	–	7.6	7.4	7.5	7.4	7.4	7.2	7.4	7.2
14	–	–	–	–	7.5	7.4	7.5	7.4	7.4	7.3	7.4	7.2
15	–	–	–	–	7.5	7.4	7.6	7.4	7.4	7.3	7.4	7.2
16	–	–	–	–	7.5	7.4	7.6	7.4	7.4	7.3	7.4	7.2
17	–	–	–	–	7.6	7.5	7.5	7.4	7.5	7.3	7.4	7.2
18	–	–	–	–	7.5	7.4	7.5	7.3	7.4	7.3	7.4	7.2
19	–	–	–	–	7.5	7.4	7.5	7.3	7.4	7.3	7.3	7.1
20	–	–	–	–	7.5	7.4	7.5	7.3	7.4	7.3	7.3	7.1
21	–	–	–	–	7.5	7.2	7.6	7.4	7.4	7.2	7.3	7.1
22	–	–	–	–	7.3	7.2	7.6	7.4	7.4	7.3	7.3	7.1
23	–	–	–	–	7.3	7.2	7.5	7.4	7.5	7.3	7.3	7.1
24	–	–	–	–	7.3	7.2	7.4	7.3	7.4	7.3	7.3	7.1
25	–	–	–	–	7.3	7.3	7.4	7.3	7.5	7.3	7.3	7.1
26	–	–	–	–	7.4	7.3	7.4	7.3	7.5	7.3	7.3	7.1
27	–	–	7.6	7.5	7.4	7.3	7.5	7.3	7.5	7.3	–	–
28	–	–	7.6	7.5	7.5	7.4	7.5	7.3	7.5	7.3	–	–
29	–	–	7.6	7.5	7.5	7.4	7.5	7.3	7.5	7.3	–	–
30	–	–	7.7	7.5	7.5	7.4	7.5	7.3	7.5	7.3	–	–
31	–	–	7.6	7.5	–	–	7.5	7.3	7.4	7.3	–	–
Month	–	–	–	–	7.6	7.2	7.6	7.1	7.5	7.2	–	–

Table 13.   Specific conductance data for USGS streamflow-gaging station 15298040, Chulitna River 5 miles above mouth, near Port Alsworth, Alaska, water years 2010 and 2011.

[**Abbreviations:** Max, maximum; Min, minimum; –, no data]

Day	Specific conductance, water, unfiltered, microsiemens per centimeter at 25 degrees Celsius, water year October 2009 to September 2010											
	April		May		June		July		August		September	
	Max	Min	Max	Min	Max	Min	Max	Min	Max	Min	Max	Min
1	–	–	–	–	66	64	80	77	61	59	69	69
2	–	–	–	–	67	66	79	77	62	61	70	69
3	–	–	–	–	67	66	79	78	63	62	71	70
4	–	–	–	–	68	66	79	78	62	61	71	70
5	–	–	–	–	67	65	79	77	61	60	70	69
6	–	–	–	–	68	65	77	74	60	60	70	69
7	–	–	–	–	69	67	75	73	60	59	70	70
8	–	–	–	–	74	69	76	74	60	58	70	69
9	–	–	–	–	74	68	76	76	60	59	70	69
10	–	–	–	–	69	69	77	75	63	60	72	70
11	–	–	–	–	69	68	75	71	61	58	76	72
12	–	–	–	–	70	69	73	71	58	58	75	74
13	–	–	–	–	70	70	74	73	61	58	75	75
14	–	–	–	–	71	70	75	72	61	59	76	75
15	–	–	–	–	71	70	73	72	61	59	76	75
16	–	–	–	–	70	68	73	72	60	59	76	75
17	–	–	–	–	73	69	73	72	59	56	76	75
18	–	–	–	–	72	68	73	72	57	55	77	76
19	–	–	–	–	73	69	72	71	60	57	77	76
20	–	–	–	–	72	68	72	71	62	60	77	77
21	–	–	–	–	72	70	71	70	64	62	78	77
22	–	–	–	–	73	72	73	71	64	63	78	78
23	–	–	–	–	74	73	75	73	64	63	81	78
24	–	–	–	–	76	74	75	74	64	64	79	78
25	–	–	–	–	76	75	75	73	66	64	79	78
26	–	–	60	59	77	76	73	64	67	66	78	78
27	–	–	60	60	78	76	66	62	68	67	79	78
28	–	–	60	58	78	77	67	63	68	68	79	78
29	–	–	62	60	79	78	67	65	69	68	–	78
30	–	–	63	62	79	78	65	60	69	69	–	–
31	–	–	65	63	–	–	60	59	70	69	–	–
Month	–	–	–	–	79	64	80	59	70	55	–	–

Table 13. Specific conductance data for USGS streamflow-gaging station 15298040, Chulitna River 5 miles above mouth, near Port Alsworth, Alaska, water years 2010 and 2011.—Continued

[**Abbreviations:** Max, maximum; Min, minimum; –, no data]

Day	Specific conductance, water, unfiltered, microsiemens per centimeter at 25 degrees Celsius, water year October 2010 to September 2011											
	April		May		June		July		August		September	
	Max	Min	Max	Min	Max	Min	Max	Min	Max	Min	Max	Min
1	–	–	–	–	79	76	69	68	74	73	73	71
2	–	–	–	–	81	71	69	69	75	71	73	71
3	–	–	–	–	77	71	69	69	71	64	73	72
4	–	–	–	–	83	77	69	67	68	64	74	72
5	–	–	–	–	84	76	67	66	67	65	73	72
6	–	–	–	–	83	77	67	66	70	65	73	72
7	–	–	–	–	83	75	68	67	67	65	73	72
8	–	–	–	–	75	72	69	68	67	65	73	71
9	–	–	–	–	88	74	70	69	65	64	72	70
10	–	–	–	–	91	87	70	69	65	64	72	70
11	–	–	–	–	91	76	69	68	67	65	72	70
12	–	–	–	–	78	74	68	68	68	66	74	70
13	–	–	–	–	76	74	68	68	69	67	72	71
14	–	–	–	–	78	72	70	68	69	68	72	70
15	–	–	–	–	74	72	72	70	73	68	74	71
16	–	–	–	–	77	74	76	71	70	69	73	71
17	–	–	–	–	77	74	73	71	73	70	77	71
18	–	–	–	–	86	75	71	69	71	71	79	74
19	–	–	–	–	86	81	70	69	71	71	77	73
20	–	–	–	–	82	76	72	70	71	69	76	73
21	–	–	–	–	76	61	73	71	71	69	74	72
22	–	–	–	–	61	59	74	73	71	70	74	71
23	–	–	–	–	65	61	75	73	72	71	76	73
24	–	–	–	–	66	65	74	70	71	71	78	72
25	–	–	–	–	67	66	72	68	72	71	78	73
26	–	–	–	–	67	66	69	68	73	72	78	73
27	–	–	67	63	67	66	71	69	73	72	–	–
28	–	–	70	67	67	66	73	71	74	72	–	–
29	–	–	70	68	67	66	73	71	75	74	–	–
30	–	–	73	70	68	67	76	72	75	74	–	–
31	–	–	76	73	–	–	75	72	75	73	–	–
Month	–	–	–	–	91	59	76	66	75	64	–	–

Table 14.   Turbidity data for USGS streamflow-gaging station 15298040, Chulitna River 5 miles above mouth, near Port Alsworth, Alaska, water years 2010 and 2011.

[**Abbreviations:** Max, maximum; Min, minimum; –, no data]

| Day | Turbidity, water, unfiltered, near Ir light-emitting diode light, 780–900 nanometers, detect angle 90 degrees formazin nephelometric units (FNU), water year October 2009 to September 2010 | | | | | | | | | | | |
| | April | | May | | June | | July | | August | | September | |
	Max	Min	Max	Min	Max	Min	Max	Min	Max	Min	Max	Min
1	–	–	–	–	6.2	3.1	4.5	3.0	12	8.6	–	–
2	–	–	–	–	4.6	3.0	5.3	3.0	12	8.5	–	–
3	–	–	–	–	6.1	2.9	3.8	3.1	12	8.0	–	–
4	–	–	–	–	6.2	3.3	4.1	3.2	20	8.6	13	3.9
5	–	–	–	–	9.9	5.2	5.0	3.2	13	9.2	8.3	3.8
6	–	–	–	–	14	3.6	5.5	3.4	13	8.3	6.2	3.8
7	–	–	–	–	6.3	3.4	5.4	3.7	11	7.4	6.1	3.9
8	–	–	–	–	5.4	3.5	5.7	3.7	10	7.1	8.8	4.1
9	–	–	–	–	7.1	3.9	5.6	4.1	11	6.8	7.9	4.8
10	–	–	–	–	6.9	3.4	5.8	4.1	9.9	7.9	6.2	3.9
11	–	–	–	–	5.0	3.0	11	4.5	40	8.1	5.1	3.0
12	–	–	–	–	5.2	2.8	9.3	5.2	48	10	3.6	2.3
13	–	–	–	–	5.2	3.0	6.6	5.2	16	8.8	3.0	2.3
14	–	–	–	–	11	3.1	8.4	5.6	17	7.3	3.9	2.2
15	–	–	–	–	7.2	3.3	9.1	5.9	20	7.5	4.3	1.7
16	–	–	–	–	8.4	3.9	8.6	6.2	25	11	2.8	1.5
17	–	–	–	–	8.0	5.7	9.6	5.9	–	10	2.4	1.5
18	–	–	–	–	9.2	5.9	8.7	5.8	–	–	2.3	1.0
19	–	–	–	–	7.4	5.4	8.8	5.9	–	–	3.2	0.8
20	–	–	–	–	9.3	5.8	10	5.9	–	–	3.0	0.7
21	–	–	–	–	7.2	4.8	12	7.9	–	–	2.4	0.6
22	–	–	–	–	8.0	3.9	8.9	5.1	–	–	2.4	0.9
23	–	–	–	–	5.2	3.3	6.7	4.4	–	–	3.2	1.3
24	–	–	–	–	5.1	3.5	8.2	4.7	–	–	4.2	1.5
25	–	–	–	–	5.2	3.2	7.3	4.9	–	–	2.8	1.3
26	–	–	5.2	3.8	4.5	2.8	23	5.3	–	–	4.2	2.3
27	–	–	4.6	3.3	3.8	2.7	20	10	–	–	7.0	3.8
28	–	–	5.1	3.6	4.8	2.8	11	7.1	–	–	12	6.5
29	–	–	5.4	3.8	4.2	2.9	10	6.8	–	–	–	–
30	–	–	5.4	3.6	4.3	2.9	15	7.8	–	–	–	–
31	–	–	5.8	3.1	–	–	17	9.7	–	–	–	–
Month	–	–	–	–	14	2.7	23	3.0	–	–	–	–

Table 14.   Turbidity data for USGS streamflow-gaging station 15298040, Chulitna River 5 miles above mouth, near Port Alsworth, Alaska, water years 2010 and 2011.—Continued

[**Abbreviations:** Max, maximum; Min, minimum; –, no data]

Day	Turbidity, water, unfiltered, near Ir light-emitting diode light, 780–900 nanometers, detect angle 90 degrees formazin nephelometric units (FNU), water year October 2010 to September 2011											
	April		May		June		July		August		September	
	Max	Min	Max	Min	Max	Min	Max	Min	Max	Min	Max	Min
1	–	–	–	–	18	1.8	10	4.1	23	15	1.7	<1.0
2	–	–	–	–	28	6.0	29	3.4	30	22	5.9	<1.0
3	–	–	–	–	7.9	2.3	9.9	3.4	–	–	1.3	<1.0
4	–	–	–	–	8.6	0.4	11	3.7	–	–	1.9	<1.0
5	–	–	–	–	16	8.0	8.5	4.2	–	–	0.8	<1.0
6	–	–	–	–	12	7.9	12	4.3	–	–	2.7	<1.0
7	–	–	–	–	19	4.6	23	4.8	–	–	4.1	<1.0
8	–	–	–	–	7.9	4.8	17	4.9	–	–	3.0	<1.0
9	–	–	–	–	16	5.3	12	3.4	–	–	9.0	0.2
10	–	–	–	–	15	4.8	19	3.9	–	–	2.8	0.7
11	–	–	–	–	8.3	4.1	13	5.3	–	–	4.1	0.1
12	–	–	–	–	12	5.0	7.5	5.4	–	–	1.3	<1.0
13	–	–	–	–	8.9	5.3	7.9	2.8	–	–	6.7	0.7
14	–	–	–	–	9.5	3.9	6.3	2.8	–	–	2.7	0.5
15	–	–	–	–	12	2.3	4.0	2.5	–	–	3.1	1.0
16	–	–	–	–	6.7	1.5	6.7	2.4	–	–	7.2	1.6
17	–	–	–	–	3.4	0.7	5.5	1.9	–	–	4.7	1.4
18	–	–	–	–	9.2	1.3	7.7	1.5	–	–	3.9	0.7
19	–	–	–	–	3.4	0.8	11	1.1	–	–	1.7	0.1
20	–	–	–	–	9.8	1.4	5.3	1.0	–	–	1.2	<1.0
21	–	–	–	–	44	8.7	2.8	0.6	–	–	7.2	<1.0
22	–	–	–	–	23	8.7	2.9	0.8	–	–	11	<1.0
23	–	–	–	–	26	6.7	7.0	2.1	–	–	5.7	<1.0
24	–	–	–	–	21	7.0	8.6	3.9	e2.0	<1.0	1.0	<1.0
25	–	–	–	–	18	7.7	13	6.1	0.7	<1.0	0.9	<1.0
26	–	–	–	–	14	6.4	12	3.0	0.4	<1.0	1.0	<1.0
27	–	–	12	5.3	11	5.4	14	6.7	1.3	<1.0	–	–
28	–	–	7.3	4.1	25	5.9	16	7.2	2.2	<1.0	–	–
29	–	–	6.2	1.7	11	7.1	18	11	0.4	<1.0	–	–
30	–	–	5.9	1.6	17	5.6	19	3.2	1.7	<1.0	–	–
31	–	–	8.7	1.8	–	–	18	11	0.9	<1.0	–	–
Month	–	–	–	–	44	0.4	29	0.6	–	–	–	–

Table 15.   Discharge data for USGS streamflow-gaging station 15298040, Chulitna River 5 miles above mouth, near Point Alsworth, Alaska, water years 2010 and 2011.

[**Abbreviations:** Max, maximum; Min, minimum; e, estimated; Acre-ft, acre-foot; Cfsm, cubic foot per second per square mile; In., inch]

Day	Discharge, cubic feet per second, water year October 2009 to September 2010 daily mean values											
	Oct.	Nov.	Dec.	Jan.	Feb.	Mar.	Apr.	May	June	July	Aug.	Sept.
1	e1,400	e1,250	e600	e430	e280	e280	e270	e1,900	1,860	1,090	4,030	3,270
2	e1,350	e1,230	e570	e420	e280	e280	e270	e2,200	1,820	1,070	3,850	3,060
3	e1,300	e1,230	e560	e420	e270	e280	e270	e2,500	1,760	1,090	3,720	2,920
4	e1,320	e1,220	e550	e420	e270	e280	e270	e2,800	1,930	1,150	3,700	2,940
5	e1,380	e1,200	e540	e420	e270	e270	e270	e4,200	2,060	1,180	3,800	3,180
6	e1,410	e1,160	e540	e430	e270	e270	e260	3,610	1,890	1,510	3,990	3,090
7	e1,500	e1,100	e540	e430	e270	e270	e260	3,320	1,800	1,520	4,460	3,200
8	1,880	e1,050	e530	e420	e260	e270	e260	3,180	1,740	1,510	4,740	3,590
9	2,700	e1,000	e530	e420	e260	e270	e260	3,120	1,720	1,460	4,600	4,150
10	2,270	e1,000	e520	e410	e260	e260	e260	3,080	1,790	1,450	4,580	3,980
11	2,140	e980	e510	e410	e260	e260	e270	2,950	1,730	1,880	5,550	3,810
12	2,260	e950	e500	e400	e260	e260	e270	2,880	1,690	1,940	5,970	3,640
13	2,270	e920	e490	e390	e270	e260	e270	2,870	1,690	1,840	5,710	3,470
14	2,190	e890	e480	e380	e270	e260	e270	2,750	1,600	1,910	5,310	3,300
15	2,150	e850	e470	e370	e280	e260	e270	2,620	1,650	1,890	4,990	3,160
16	2,100	e810	e460	e360	e280	e260	e270	2,610	1,700	1,830	5,110	3,010
17	2,030	e780	e450	e350	e290	e250	e270	2,510	1,670	1,760	5,470	2,870
18	1,960	e760	e440	e340	e290	e260	e290	2,410	1,640	1,740	5,900	2,740
19	1,900	e740	e430	e330	e290	e260	e320	2,310	1,570	1,810	5,450	2,620
20	1,840	e720	e420	e320	e300	e270	e340	2,430	1,570	1,910	5,080	2,500
21	1,790	e700	e410	e310	e300	e270	e360	2,660	1,520	2,660	4,780	2,400
22	1,730	e690	e410	e300	e300	e270	e390	2,520	1,450	2,560	4,530	2,300
23	1,710	e680	e410	e300	e290	e280	e420	2,360	1,380	2,470	4,330	2,230
24	1,770	e670	e420	e300	e290	e280	e460	2,280	1,340	2,590	4,050	2,150
25	1,840	e650	e420	e290	e290	e280	e550	2,230	1,300	2,680	3,790	2,070
26	1,780	e640	e430	e290	e290	e280	e650	2,200	1,280	3,370	3,560	1,980
27	1,740	e630	e430	e290	e290	e280	e820	2,190	1,250	3,800	3,470	1,900
28	1,620	e620	e440	e280	e280	e280	e1,000	2,150	1,230	3,560	3,510	1,830
29	e1,500	e610	e440	e280	–	e270	e1,250	2,080	1,190	3,590	3,390	1,820
30	e1,400	e600	e440	e280	–	e270	e1,570	2,050	1,140	4,020	3,210	1,930
31	e1,320	–	e430	e280	–	e270	–	1,960	–	4,280	3,210	–
Total	55,550	26,330	14,810	11,070	7,810	8,360	12,960	80,930	47,960	67,120	137,840	85,110
Mean	1,792	878	478	357	279	270	432	2,611	1,599	2,165	4,446	2,837
Max	2,700	1,250	600	430	300	280	1,570	4,200	2,060	4,280	5,970	4,150
Min	1,300	600	410	280	260	250	260	1,900	1,140	1,070	3,210	1,820
Acre-ft	110,200	52,230	29,380	21,960	15,490	16,580	25,710	160,500	95,130	133,100	273,400	168,800
Cfsm	1.60	0.78	0.43	0.32	0.25	0.24	0.39	2.33	1.43	1.93	3.97	2.53
In.	1.85	0.87	0.49	0.37	0.26	0.28	0.43	2.69	1.59	2.23	4.58	2.83

Table 15.   Discharge data for USGS streamflow-gaging station 15298040, Chulitna River 5 miles above mouth, near Point Alsworth, Alaska, water years 2010 and 2011.—Continued

[**Abbreviations:** Max, maximum; Min, minimum; e, estimated; Acre-ft, acre-foot; Cfsm, cubic foot per second per square mile; In., inch]

Day	Discharge, cubic feet per second, water year October 2010 to September 2011 daily mean values											
	Oct.	Nov.	Dec.	Jan.	Feb.	Mar.	Apr.	May	June	July	Aug.	Sept.
1	2,040	e1,400	e690	e405	e365	e335	e340	e3,900	2,880	2,580	2,700	3,280
2	2,050	e1,380	e680	e410	e360	e335	e340	e4,650	3,290	2,510	2,890	3,130
3	2,150	e1,360	e670	e415	e360	e335	e340	4,090	2,880	2,560	3,750	3,170
4	2,240	e1,300	e660	e415	e355	e335	e345	3,930	2,700	2,810	3,710	3,220
5	2,270	e1,200	e640	e420	e355	e335	e345	3,800	2,640	2,870	4,070	3,160
6	2,190	e1,100	e630	e420	e355	e330	e345	3,730	2,580	2,630	3,960	3,080
7	2,120	e1,020	e610	e415	e360	e330	e345	3,630	2,500	2,470	4,160	3,030
8	2,060	e950	e590	e415	e360	e330	e345	3,440	2,490	2,360	4,200	3,040
9	2,020	e900	e580	e405	e365	e330	e350	3,390	2,450	2,240	4,550	3,000
10	1,960	e870	e570	e400	e365	e330	e350	3,400	2,340	2,280	4,710	2,910
11	1,890	e860	e565	e400	e360	e330	e345	3,180	2,200	2,280	4,440	2,820
12	1,820	e850	e560	e395	e360	e325	e345	2,960	2,140	2,460	4,260	2,720
13	1,760	e840	e550	e395	e355	e325	e345	2,890	2,080	2,560	4,300	2,630
14	1,640	e820	e545	e390	e355	e325	e345	2,850	2,060	2,410	4,070	2,530
15	e1,620	e800	e540	e390	e350	e325	e350	2,690	2,000	2,340	3,840	2,430
16	1,610	e790	e530	e385	e350	e325	e355	2,650	1,920	2,280	3,640	2,380
17	1,580	e780	e520	e385	e350	e325	e360	2,530	1,830	2,250	3,450	2,330
18	1,620	e770	e500	e380	e350	e325	e365	2,480	1,760	2,660	3,290	2,280
19	1,580	e760	e490	e380	e350	e325	e385	2,540	1,710	2,550	3,230	2,210
20	1,530	e750	e480	e375	e345	e330	e400	2,550	2,220	2,370	3,610	2,160
21	1,490	e740	e465	e375	e345	e330	e450	2,490	3,940	2,290	3,520	2,180
22	1,450	e740	e460	e370	e345	e330	e500	2,500	4,060	2,260	3,360	2,180
23	1,470	e750	e455	e370	e345	e330	e560	2,470	3,710	2,230	3,330	2,130
24	1,470	e770	e445	e370	e340	e335	e700	2,410	3,440	2,690	3,220	2,100
25	1,470	e760	e430	e375	e340	e335	e1,200	2,280	3,280	2,970	3,090	2,050
26	1,440	e750	e425	e370	e340	e340	e2,500	2,360	3,170	3,030	2,990	2,010
27	1,390	e740	e410	e370	e340	e340	e4,400	2,390	2,990	2,930	2,890	1,970
28	1,500	e730	e405	e365	e340	e340	e4,200	2,440	2,950	2,900	2,820	1,910
29	1,590	e720	e405	e370	–	e345	e3,900	2,460	2,880	3,000	2,710	1,850
30	1,540	e700	e400	e370	–	e345	e3,750	2,460	2,720	2,860	2,650	1,790
31	e1,460	–	e400	e365	–	e345	–	2,560	–	2,730	2,950	–
Total	54,020	26,900	16,300	12,065	9,860	10,300	29,200	92,100	79,810	79,360	110,360	75,680
Mean	1,743	897	526	389	352	332	973	2,971	2,660	2,560	3,560	2,523
Max	2,270	1,400	690	420	365	345	4,400	4,650	4,060	3,030	4,710	3,280
Min	1,390	700	400	365	340	325	340	2,280	1,710	2,230	2,650	1,790
Acre-ft	107,100	53,360	32,330	23,930	19,560	20,430	57,920	182,700	158,300	157,400	218,900	150,100
Cfsm	1.56	0.80	0.47	0.35	0.31	0.30	0.87	2.65	2.38	2.29	3.18	2.25
In.	1.79	0.89	0.54	0.40	0.33	0.34	0.97	3.06	2.65	2.64	3.67	2.51

www.ingramcontent.com/pod-product-compliance
Lightning Source LLC
Chambersburg PA
CBHW080352290526
45791CB00009BA/2843